M000195979

To Richard Stockhom
with fond memories
of old time

[signature]

ALL RIGHT
LET THEM COME

John Guilford Earnest

ALL RIGHT LET THEM COME

The Civil War Diary

of an

East Tennessee Confederate

EDITED BY
CHARLES SWIFT NORTHEN III

Voices of the Civil War
Peter S. Carmichael, Series Editor

The University of Tennessee Press
Knoxville

THE VOICES OF THE CIVIL WAR series makes available a variety of primary source materials that illuminate issues on the battlefield, the home front, and the western front, as well as other aspects of this historic era. The series contextualizes the personal accounts within the framework of the latest scholarship and expands established knowledge by offering new perspectives, new materials, and new voices.

Copyright © 2003 by The University of Tennessee Press / Knoxville.
All Rights Reserved. Manufactured in the United States of America.
First Edition.

Frontispiece: John Guilford Earnest. Photographer unknown, undated.

This book is printed on acid-free paper.

Library of Congress Cataloging-in-Publication Data

Earnest, John Guilford, d. 1932.
All right let them come: the Civil War diary of an East Tennessee
Confederate/edited by Charles Swift Northen III.—1st ed.
    p. cm.   — (Voices of the Civil War)

ISBN: 1-57233-233-6 (cl.: alk. paper)

  1. Earnest, John Guilford, d. 1932—Diaries.
  2. Confederate States of America. Army. Tennessee Infantry Regiment, 60th.
  3. Soldiers—Tennessee, East—Diaries.
  4. Tennessee, East—History—Civil War, 1861–1865—Personal narratives.
  5. United States—History—Civil War, 1861–1865—Personal narratives,
     Confederate.
  6. Vicksburg (Miss.)—History—Siege, 1863—Personal narratives, Confederate.
  I. Northen, Charles Swift III.
  II. Title.
  III. Series: Voices of the Civil War series.

E579.5 60th .E37 2003
973.7'82—dc21   2003007244

THUMP! THUMP! An old man, feeling left out of the gay chatter of his family scattered about the room, lifts his hand and lets it fall upon the small table beside his chair. THUMP! A young boy playing on the floor nearby looks up at his grandfather. The Civil War veteran has captured an audience. THUMP! "Sounds like thunder," the old campaigner says. THUMP! "No, it sounds like the guns of Vicksburg!" Thus would begin another tale of adventure in the late war.

The teller of the tales, Dr. John Guilford Earnest, formerly lieutenant in the Confederate army, died in 1932. His grandson, my father, recently followed him. The stories told many years ago have long been forgotten. But my great-grandfather left something more than a fond memory. He left a diary.

That diary and many other documents and artifacts of the family history were carefully collected and preserved by my father. Therefore, it is right that this edition be dedicated to the memory of Charles Swift Northen Jr.

Contents

Foreword

JOHN EARNEST came from Unionist East Tennessee, but he witnessed the outbreak of war from one of the most pro-Confederate universities in the South—Virginia's Emory and Henry. It is likely that Earnest developed his pro-Confederate views while studying at that institution, for many of his peers had repeatedly clashed with the pro-Unionist faculty after Lincoln was elected in the fall of 1860. When Earnest returned to his native Greene County in May of 1861, he found public opinion overwhelmingly against secession. Unlike most of the county's residents, Earnest came from a prestigious slave-owning family. His grandfather owned fifteen African Americans and had amassed a fortune of more than $97,000. Even a material stake in the institution of slavery and an education in the school of Southern rights did not inspire Earnest to enlist. Not until the fall of 1862, with the immediate threat of conscription, did this young man join some of the last Confederate troops raised in East Tennessee.

Unfortunately, little is known regarding Earnest's decision to enlist, but one can only imagine that it must have been a torturous one. On October 24, 1862, not long after his enlistment, Earnest penned his first diary entry. He continued to chronicle his military activities until his unit surrendered at Vicksburg on July 4, 1863. Earnest rarely explored ideological issues or commented on the politics of the day. Little is said about how the war brought bitter fighting and social turmoil to his divided East Tennessee. Nor did he use his journal for therapeutic purposes, to either liberate himself of painful emotions or to relate a horrible event experienced in combat. Rather, Earnest used his diary to record the daily struggles of being a soldier in the field. To his credit, there is not a hint of romanticism in his writings. Earnest provides a gritty, realistic look inside the Confederate army. There are plenty of details involving guard duty, foraging, and drill, but he writes of these ordinary activities with a wonderful sense of humor. His account of being attacked by a mosquito is priceless. Earnest described the vicious insect as having "claws like a ground hog and a bill half as long as a sergeant's sword." Before the mosquito could "run his bill" through the young soldier's neck, he yelled "murder! murder!" which scared the "old skeeter" off.

All Right Let Them Come offers one of the finest Confederate accounts from a participant in the siege of Vicksburg. Earnest conveys the misery of those who languished in trenches, surviving on a sparse diet that apparently included rats, while surrounded by an unrelenting enemy that eventually squeezed the life out of the Confederate army. He did not overly dramatize the heroics of either his fellow soldiers or Vicksburg's civilians. Earnest was defiant to the end, but without the highly charged rhetoric or the histrionics one might expect from a Confederate facing inevitable defeat. His daily entries capture the rhythm of the siege as soldiers moved in and out of the lines, finding peace and a degree of solitude for a few days, before returning to the earthworks and life under enemy fire. Charles S. Northen III worked closely with the late Dr. Frank Byrne in bringing John Guilford Earnest's diary to print. This fine manuscript is one of the last titles that Dr. Byrne shepherded to publication as part of the Voices of the Civil War Series that he inaugurated and so skillfully developed.

Peter S. Carmichael
University of North Carolina
at Greensboro

Preface

In the 1950s, when I was headed for college and considering a major in history, my father showed me the diary his grandfather, John G. Earnest, had kept during the Civil War. I transcribed it for him, and for the first time he was able to enjoy reading the entire work. Later, he gave the diary to me in return for my pledge to prepare it for publication. I only regret that this edition did not appear before his death in 1997.

But it is not only a sense of filial duty that led me to this work. In fact, the diary sheds some light on specific points that will be of interest to serious students of the Civil War.

The plan of this work is straightforward. It is intended to be a careful edition of an interesting diary. The added commentary on the progress of the war and other matters is not meant to be a definitive study, but simply an effort to place John Earnest's writing in a context where it may be more easily understood.

Before presenting the diary itself, I have provided a brief biography of John Earnest to set the work in the personal context of what must have been a difficult decision to enlist. Next, there is a biographical sketch of Earnest's brigade commander, John Crawford Vaughn. Vaughn is not frequently mentioned in the diary, but clearly his leadership was a significant influence on John Earnest, who followed him to the final surrender in 1865. As will be shown, General

Vaughn has been widely criticized for the poor performance of the troops he led. Nevertheless, his soldiers seem to have been loyal to him. This sketch is by no means a thorough study of Vaughn's life. However, it may be of value since as far as I know the only other modern biographies of Vaughn are the brief commentaries in standard compilations of Civil War generals.

In the course of the chapters on Earnest and on Vaughn, the reader's attention is drawn to three aspects of Civil War history about which John Earnest's diary directly or indirectly comments.

First is the question of the loyalty and commitment of East Tennessee Confederates. The people of the region were sharply divided, with a majority favoring the North. The poor performance of East Tennessee's Confederate troops was assumed at the time to stem from this divided loyalty. That may be, but there is no evidence on this point in the diary. Earnest offers little comment about his own convictions and almost nothing about the sentiments of his fellow soldiers. Instead, his narrative suggests the inference that a contributing weakness may have been a lack of training and discipline.

The inadequacy of the Confederate railway system is not a new discovery. However, the diary's account of the long journey from Knoxville to Jackson, Mississippi, is a graphic illustration of the transportation difficulties that hampered the South's war effort.

Last is the question of food for the soldiers in Vicksburg during the siege. The Earnest diary indicates that shortages of many edibles appeared well before the siege began. The final diary entry includes mention of eating rats. The scattered references in other diaries and memoirs to the necessity of eating rats have been dismissed as a misunderstanding of the Louisiana soldiers' inclusion of muskrats in their diet. However, it seems unlikely that the diarist from East Tennessee would not know a rat when he saw one.[1]

If this mention of eating rats is indeed rare, it raises the question of whether the entry containing it is contemporaneous with the rest of the diary. The only comment in the diary that is clearly a later addition is an interlining at March 7, describing his illness: "Turned out be a case of catarrhal jaundice." Here the experienced doctor, with a different ink and more mature hand, is correcting a youthful diagnosis.

The final entry, containing the reference to rats, is not so certainly a late one. Its content is clearly that of a final summary. It is written on an end page of the book, which, unlike those preceding, is unlined, and the text tends to slant slightly down from left to right. The script might be judged a trifle less steady than that preceding it, but it is far from the wavering scrawl of an aged hand. Unlike the March 7 addition, the ink has faded to a shade of brown matching the rest of the text. There can be no certainty, but a reasonable conclusion is that shortly after July 4, 1863, Earnest, surrendered, paroled, weakened by the rigors of the siege, and on the penultimate page of his only available book, decided to close his diary with this summary.

All in all, the Earnest diary is a worthwhile contribution to the historiography of the Civil War.

John Earnest wrote in a small (9½" by 7 ½") composition book that has survived to this day with remarkably little wear and tear. His was a careful script that is generally easy to read. The spelling of some personal names has, however, been difficult to decipher. Names of fellow soldiers have been checked against other sources where possible, but names of some of the families with whom Earnest visited may be incorrectly copied. Where a corrected spelling of a name is available, it is supplied in the commentary, but without a correction in the text.

On the inside cover and first page of the book, Earnest has written his name several times, either merely doodling or practicing to determine his favored formal signature. These inscriptions place him variously at his hometown of Fullens, Tennessee, at Emory and Henry College, and at Vicksburg. The ones that are dated range from January 1859 to March 1863.

These jottings clearly indicate that the volume was originally a notebook used at college. In fact, a number of pages have been cut out of the front of the book so that the diary begins on a new leaf after the signatures. This raises the possibility that the notes on Latin and Greek appearing after the entries of March 3 and April

28 were recorded at college and not in camp at Vicksburg. However, they appear well into the text, and of course in the same hand, so that either interpretation is possible.

In preparing the text, my goal has been to present it as nearly as possible as it was written. The grammar and spelling of the original have been retained, but without distracting use of the term *sic*. Earnest's punctuation is surprisingly formal for a diary. Nevertheless, marks have occasionally been added as an aid to understanding. It was his consistent practice to place punctuation outside of final quotation marks. This practice has not been retained.

In the preparation of this book I have been aided by many people, some of whom I am sure that I will, to my regret, fail to mention here.

First on my list to thank is my wife, Betty. In addition to general comfort and support, she undertook to help in deciphering difficult parts of the text and in correcting my several drafts.

My daughter, Margaret Allen Price, once an editor and now an entrepreneur, used her old skills to review the text and contributed many improvements.

Much of my research on the diary was done at the Birmingham Public Library. The library's Tutwiler Collection of Southern History and Literature is a magnificent resource. I greatly appreciate the help of the head of the collection, Yvonne Crumpler, and her associates, Mary Beth Newbill, Jim Pate, and Ron Joullian. Their patience and skill in guiding me was invaluable.

Many others, especially the following, were helpful to my research: Darla Brock of the Tennessee State Library and Archives; W. Todd Groce at the Georgia Historical Society in Savannah; Ned Irwin, university archivist, East Tennessee State University; and Terence J. Winschel, historian, Vicksburg National Military Park.

A number of people read my manuscript and made helpful comments. Among them are the late Frank L. Byrne, R. Tracy McKenzie, and Henry E. Simpson.

At the University of Tennessee Press, I especially appreciate the support and guidance of Joyce Harrison and Stan Ivester.

Many thanks to Dr. Robert Rhea Earnest, who gave to me the photograph of John G. Earnest used here as the frontispiece. I was introduced to Dr. Earnest by David L. Taylor, of Costa Mesa, California, who was a direct help to me in other ways as well. David is an Earnest descendant who has developed an extensive genealogy of the family. Anyone interested in knowing more about the Earnests of East Tennessee could do no better than to call on him.

PART I

Biographies

John Guilford Earnest

JOHN EARNEST was away at school when the war began. The first in his line to attend college, he had traveled from his Greene County home in East Tennessee to western Virginia to study at Emory and Henry College.

When the first shots of the Civil War were fired at Charleston, South Carolina, on April 12, 1861, Emory and Henry students became restless. By early May, they could no longer be restrained. Even the seniors, who had completed class work and were just days away from receiving their degrees, would not wait. The student body withdrew, and John Earnest, a graduate without a diploma, returned home to celebrate his nineteenth birthday on May 16, 1861, and to consider the future.[1]

After some delay, he chose to join the Confederate army, but the decision could not have been an easy one. In many parts of the South, public sentiment was such that young men flocked to the Confederate banner almost without thinking about it. Where John Earnest lived, the course was not so clear.

East Tennessee, although geographically part of the South, was in many ways not typical of the region. Ever since colonial times, East Tennesseans had seen themselves as different, even to the attempt to form the separate state of Franklin in the 1780s.

The region of East Tennessee consists of a great, hilly valley, running roughly north to south, bordered on the east by the Great Smoky Mountains of the Appalachian Range, and subdivided by several ridges into many other valleys. On its western side, the Great Valley is separated from the rest of Tennessee by the crest of the Cumberland Plateau. Several rivers flow into the valley at different points, finally coming together to form the Tennessee River.

As railroads developed, they generally ran north and south through the valley, exiting at the upper end into western Virginia and at the lower end continuing south into Georgia or going through Chattanooga to various points, including northwest to Nashville. This did little to bind East Tennessee to the rest of the state.

A slaveholding economy never took hold, primarily because the thin and rocky soil of the mountainous region did not lend itself easily to agriculture on a large scale.[2] In 1860 only one farm household in ten owned slaves. Slaves made up only 9.2 percent of East Tennessee's population in 1860, while they accounted for 29 percent of the population in Middle Tennessee and 33.5 percent in West Tennessee. The result was that, while most East Tennesseans probably did not object to slavery per se, they had little reason to favor promotion of its growth in the South, or its expansion to new territories. And fighting to preserve the institution did not prove to be a popular cause.[3]

One result of the move toward secession and war was to rekindle the consciousness of separateness that was already firmly embedded in the culture of East Tennessee. Many in the region believed that the slaveholders of Middle and West Tennessee were pursuing a course that was of no benefit to the East.

William G. "Parson" Brownlow combined evangelistic fervor with a flair for the written and spoken word to become a leading Unionist spokesman in the region. But he probably represented more than just convinced Unionists when he wrote on January 26, 1861, "We are a grain-growing and stock raising people, and we can conduct a cheap government and live independently inhabiting the Switzerland of America."[4]

It was in this spirit that East Tennesseans went to the polls on June 8, 1861, to vote on a secession resolution. The results reflected the heritage of isolation from the rest of the state. Western and Middle Tennessee, respectively, voted only 17 percent and 12 percent against secession. East Tennessee voters were overwhelmingly Unionist, with 68 percent voting against secession.[5]

John Earnest's native Greene County was one of the largest slaveholding counties in the region. Nevertheless, 78 percent of the county's voters rejected secession.[6] Therefore, as Earnest considered his decision, history, geography, and the strong force of public opinion all seemed to be arrayed against the Confederacy.

And then there was the family to consider. John's father, Nicholas W. Earnest, age forty-four in 1860, was the local agent for the East Tennessee and Virginia Railroad, which had been completed on May 14, 1858. He reported to the census taker real and personal property with a total value of $45,000, including one male slave, age twenty-six. Nicholas was a widower, his wife, Martha, having died in 1847. In 1861, there were three living children of the marriage, John, born 1842; Mariah Ruth, born 1844; and Rebecca Catherine, born 1846.

Not too far away lived John's grandfather, Peter, who was eighty-four in 1861. Peter was born February 27, 1777, in North Carolina. In April 1777, his father Henry moved his wife and eight children to East Tennessee, where three more children were born. By 1860, of Peter's twelve children he had four sons and three daughters living. He lived on the family farm with his son, Benjamin F. Earnest.

Peter reported to the census taker in 1860 that he had real and personal property worth $97,000, including fifteen slaves. This was a considerable fortune when compared with average family wealth of $2,830 in East Tennessee, and even to the average of $7,130 in prosperous West Tennessee.[7]

In this deeply divided region, John was faced with the need to reconcile many conflicting arguments for and against actively joining the Southern cause. No records survive to help us follow John Earnest's thoughts from the time of his hasty departure from

Emory and Henry College in May 1861 to his late enlistment in the Confederate army in September 1862. However, it is possible to imagine some of the forces pulling him one way or the other.

Economic considerations were certainly important. The family was prosperous well above the average and had a large slavehold-ing. If the North were to prevail, much of the Earnest wealth could be lost.

The influence of community sentiment probably was felt on both sides of the issue at different times. The first wave of enthu-siasm led to many enlistments in the months after Fort Sumter, yet John Earnest was not among them. And by November 4, 1861, popular support for the Confederacy had waned to the extent that J. G. M. Ramsey, a leading secessionist in Knoxville, was moved to write to Jefferson Davis for help. He wanted Col. John Vaughn and his Tennessee troops returned from Virginia, not only for the defense of the valley but also in the hope that the example of these "brave men" would "excite (revive is not the word) the spirit of vol-unteering, which I am humiliated to say is very low."[8]

The situation in East Tennessee from 1861 to 1865 has been described as "a civil war within a civil war," because of the deeply divided loyalties there.[9] In that environment, John certainly had to think of the safety of his family. Surrounded by Unionist neighbors, who might also be jealous of the family's wealth, what might hap-pen if he left to fight for a cause that was locally unpopular? Should he stay home to protect his father and his young sisters?

No doubt, passage of the conscription law in April 1862 also weighed on John. When he enlisted in the fall of 1862, he was among the men who made up the last units of volunteers organized in East Tennessee. Many observers at the time and later believed that these three regiments, which made up the brigade of Gen. John C. Vaughn, would never have materialized had it not been for the threat of the draft.[10]

On September 9, 1862, A. F. Naff wrote to Col. John H. Crawford, who was to command John Earnest's regiment, resign-ing the commission Crawford had offered him. Naff's mission had been to enlist volunteers in Greene County. He informed Crawford that "he had found he could not succeed," and mentioned in passing, "The Earnest boys say they are not going unless conscription comes."[11] By the end of the month, the Earnests had changed their minds, but not many of their neighbors joined them. The regiment in which they enrolled was organized in adjoining Washington County but included a few Greene County boys.

However, there was surely more to John Earnest's decision than a fear of the draft. He could have afforded to hire a substitute, or he could simply have tried to dodge conscription by fleeing north to Kentucky. Certainly he had contemporaries in Greene County doing one or the other. But John's fourteen months of deliberation produced more than just a perfunctory enlistment to avoid another evil. In those months he had somehow matured a conviction that would keep him in the dwindling army until the end, in April 1865.

John Earnest's diary tells us little of his doubts or concerns about home. His diary is a narrative, and only rarely a place for introspection. Nevertheless, when he does express his feelings, he shows himself to be dedicated, even defiant, as when he writes on April 30, 1863, as the Yankees drew closer to Vicksburg, "All right let them come."

The diary opens with an entry on October 24, 1862, shortly after the brigade was organized, but before it was formally mustered into the Confederate army on November 7. The final entry describes the privations suffered before the surrender of Vicksburg on July 4, 1863.

John Earnest's regiment, the Sixtieth Tennessee Infantry (first known as the Seventy-ninth), was organized on October 1, 1862, from companies that had been enrolled in August and September, and was mustered into service at Haynesville, Tennessee (now part of Johnson City), on November 7, 1862. The regiment was commanded by Col. John H. Crawford with Lt. Col. Nathan Gregg and Maj. James A. Rhea.

Major Rhea had been wounded at Shiloh on April 8, 1862. According to one source, he convalesced for four months, "finally rose from his bed of suffering," and began the organization of the Sixtieth Regiment. He was elected major and subsequently promoted to lieutenant colonel.[12]

Earnest enrolled on September 27, 1862, and that day was appointed assistant commissary of Company K. The regiment, along with the Sixty-first and Sixty-second, organized at the same time, was assigned to the command of Brig. Gen. John Crawford Vaughn. Vaughn's brigade was promptly transferred to Mississippi, where it took part in the campaign and siege of Vicksburg.

With its defeat and resultant losses at the battle of the Big Black River on May 17, 1863, Vaughn's brigade was finished as an effective fighting force. As Earnest reports on his regiment, "only two companies (ours, K, and Captain Bachman's, G) escaped, together with a few stragglers. The rest were all killed or captured."

The troops remaining after the surrender of Vicksburg on July 4, 1863, were directed to return to East Tennessee to await exchange. The journey back cannot have been easy. One veteran remembered that he started "afoot with rations from the Federal Army. 3 days rations. Then begged our way home."[13]

The exact dates of exchange varied and John Earnest's exchange date is not known. Some officers and men may have been exchanged as early as September 1863. Colonel Rose of the Sixty-first Tennessee wrote that at least some of his men were not exchanged until June 27, 1864.[14] It seems likely that Earnest was exchanged at least as early as March 1864, but whatever the date, when he marched off to join the other veterans, he did not resume his diary. He left no record of the remainder of his service.

There is one, indirect, indication of his activity late in the war. The Colt 36 revolver he brought home from the war has been handed down in his family. This pistol was originally issued to the Tenth Michigan Volunteer Cavalry in 1864.[15] In the course of a dispatch from "Headquarters Forces East Tennessee" dated October 21, 1864, General Vaughn reports, "We captured 1 lieutenant and 15 of the Tenth Michigan last evening."[16] That may have been the occasion that armed John Earnest for the rest of his service.

Assumptions aside, all that is certain about this period is that John Earnest served steadfastly until the end of the war, as far as we know with personal honor, but certainly in a brigade that was without glory. He ended the war as a second lieutenant, the position to which he was elected in March 1863. What remained of the Sixtieth Tennessee surrendered at Christiansburg, Virginia, on April 12, 1865.[17]

After the war ended, John Earnest wasted little time before beginning to build a new life. By the fall of 1865, he had enrolled in Jefferson Medical College in Philadelphia, Pennsylvania. One historian describes the education of physicians in the 1860s as being somewhat less than exacting: "medical school training was a two-year curriculum in which the second year was but a repetition of the first. Mastering what was known of medicine in the mid-nineteenth century could be learned in 12 months of study."[18]

Dr. John G. Earnest's first license states that he was residing at New Castle, Craig County, Virginia, and grants him the right to practice there from May 1, 1866 to May 1, 1867. By 1868, Dr. Earnest was practicing in East Tennessee, and on October 13 of that year he married Martha Amelia Moffett in New Market. Their first child, Nora Gordon Earnest, was born there on July 23, 1869. There were four other children, all of whom lived to be adults but who died without issue.

Nora Earnest married Charles Swift Northen in Atlanta on October 25, 1892. The wedding was held at the Governor's Mansion in Atlanta, courtesy of the groom's uncle, Gov. William Jonathan Northen. Nora Northen was well known in the Atlanta of her time. In 1927 the Atlanta Chamber of Commerce awarded three Certificates of Distinguished Achievement, one to the then president of the Atlanta Art Association, another to William B. Hartsfield, later mayor of Atlanta, and the third to Mrs. Northen, cited as "Godmother to youth—good angel of the sick and bereaved, and universally loved as 'Miss Nora.'"[19]

Following what may have been a pattern for ex-Confederates who felt unwelcome at home in East Tennessee, Dr. Earnest moved to Newnan, Georgia, in 1872. His former commanding officer, John Vaughn, also stayed only a few years in Tennessee, then moved to Georgia and died there in 1875. One East Tennessee Confederate, Capt. Reuben G. Clark, in describing the postwar period, commented that "one style of amusement indulged in by the Union people was to horsewhip Rebels who had returned to their homes unarmed and helpless. These lawless acts of oppression drove many of the best citizens out of the country, and today [1891] East Tennessee Confederates are scattered over every state in the Union."[20]

It is doubtful that John Earnest was threatened by violence, since he did not open a practice in East Tennessee until 1868, after tempers had begun to cool. Nevertheless, his grandfather, Peter had died in 1862, and his father Nicholas in 1866. His sister Mariah married in 1867, and Rebecca in 1872. Rebecca's marriage may have been the event that released John to move to a more hospitable region.[21]

Dr. Earnest's ledger from his practice in Newnan survives. In 1874, his typical charge for a day visit was $1.50; night visits could be as high as $2.50. By 1878, when the ledger ends, his standard daytime charge had risen to $2.50. Moreover, his payment was often in kind. Two bills, for $6 and $2, were "paid by pig." One hopes there was a considerable difference in the size of the pigs. Even with five children in the family, Mrs. Earnest may have been challenged by an October 1878 payment "by 54 pumpkins."

Newnan, about forty-five miles southwest of Atlanta, was even in the 1870s losing population to its nearby rival. In the 1870 Census, Newnan had a population of 2,564. By 1880, Newnan was down to 2,006, much smaller than Atlanta's 37,409, and Dr. Earnest followed others and moved to the larger city in 1881.

He apparently wasted no time before associating himself with modern technology. The Atlanta Telephonic Exchange, publishing a one-page directory of "Subscribers Connected to October 21, 1881," listed John G. Earnest as the only doctor among the grand total of 123 subscribers.[22]

Speed in transportation as well as communication was important to the energetic doctor. An article about early Atlanta history in the *Atlanta Journal and Constitution* notes: "William D. Alexander, an Atlanta bicycle dealer, ordered three steam-driven automobiles early in 1901. These were the first factory-built cars to reach Atlanta. One of the two he offered for sale was purchased by Dr. John G. Earnest."[23]

Dr. Earnest practiced medicine in Atlanta until he was well into his seventies. On March 19, 1917, the Atlanta medical profession celebrated his fifty years as a practitioner with a gala banquet.

The aged Confederate veteran died October 8, 1932. Three years before his death, he made what was perhaps his last extended trip away from home, traveling back to western Virginia. There, sitting on the stage with the Class of 1929, at the age of eighty-seven, John Guilford Earnest at last received his degree from Emory and Henry College.

John C. Vaughn
and His Brigade

JOHN CRAWFORD VAUGHN was the embodiment of some of the major strengths and weaknesses of the Confederate States at war. He was personally brave in battle and stubbornly combative against over-whelming numbers and resources. He was also irredeemably inept at meeting the disciplinary and organizational challenges posed by large-scale warfare. He was a devoted defender of the Confederacy, whose contribution to the cause was limited by minimal military training. The record of his service provides little evidence of his ability to learn from experience. Nevertheless, it also shows clearly his bravery and firm dedication. There can have been few others who were earlier, or more clearly, committed to fighting, or who persevered more nearly to the end of the war than John Vaughn.

Vaughn was born in East Tennessee on February 24, 1824. He volunteered for service in the Mexican War and served as captain in the Fifth Tennessee Volunteers, 1847 to 1848. After the war he ventured to California to try his luck in the gold rush. Returning to Sweetwater, in Monroe County, he became a merchant and an active participant in community affairs. He held several minor elective offices, and at the time of the 1860 Census was sheriff of Monroe County.

He was apparently industrious enough to turn his hand to any small job that might profit him. In 1860, he was a census taker, compiling at least the Slave Schedule for Monroe County. He recorded his own name first, as the owner of one male, age thirty-five. Anyone who has tried to read the manuscript census records would praise the work of John Vaughn. His script is bold, clear, and well defined.

On April 12, 1861, Vaughn was in Charleston, South Carolina, and witnessed the shelling of Fort Sumter. Returning to Tennessee, he raised a company of volunteers in Monroe County and led it to Knoxville to join with others.

Since Tennessee was still a part of the Union (the state did not vote to leave the Union until June 8, 1861), Vaughn led the eager troops to Virginia. They were mustered into the Confederate army at Lynchburg on June 6, 1861, and John Crawford Vaughn was elected colonel of the Third Tennessee Volunteers, the first Confederate regiment raised in East Tennessee.

The Tennessee volunteers were assigned to Gen. Joseph E. Johnston, then stationed at Harpers Ferry. On June 21, 1861, Gen. Robert E. Lee wrote to Johnston, "In relation to the two regiments sent you, one from Georgia and one from Tennessee . . . [these] were selected by the President to be added to your command because they were thought to be fully equipped and in a good state of discipline . . . He is grieved at your report of the inefficient state of the Tennessee regiment."[1]

Although the regiment had been mustered in barely three weeks earlier, many others to which it could be compared were also new, so this early criticism of Vaughn was not a good omen. Nevertheless, perhaps the highest commendation received by Vaughn in his military career came to him for his action while attached to the Harpers Ferry command.

On July 19, 1861, Vaughn marched his soldiers thirty-six miles in sixteen hours, routed Federal troops defending the railroad bridge at New Creek, Virginia, and burned the bridge. This interrupted traffic on the Baltimore and Ohio Railroad and resulted in the capture of two pieces of artillery, the first taken by the Confederates in the field. President Jefferson Davis congratulated General Johnston "on the brilliant movement of Vaughn's command in breaking the line of the B & O."[2]

The Third Tennessee served under Gen. E. Kirby Smith during the campaign and battle of Bull Run in July 1861, where it was the only Tennessee unit to take an active part in the battle. Again, evidence of relaxed discipline appeared. And here, perhaps, Kirby Smith began to develop the low opinion of East Tennesseans that dominated his thinking when he later commanded that region.

McHenry Howard, whose First Maryland fought beside the Third Tennessee at Bull Run, considered the Tennesseans to be "good material for soldiers" but also noted that when a visitor was challenged as he entered the regiment's camp, "he was in the next breath directed where to go to get the best cakes or liquor."[3]

In the spring of 1862, Colonel Vaughn was ordered back to East Tennessee. His duty, as it had been a year earlier, was to enlist new troops for the Confederacy. This time, however, the task was not as easy. Recruiting was slow, but the fault lay not with John Vaughn but with the circumstances surrounding the effort.

Geography, demographics, and the course of economic development all worked to differentiate East Tennessee and divide people's loyalties. This division of sentiment had the obvious result of reducing the portion of the male population that was open to voluntary enlistment in the Confederate army. There was also a related effect among those who were Confederate sympathizers. Even if they wished to enlist, Confederate supporters wanted the assurance that they would not be ordered to serve in other regions. In addition to repelling Yankee invaders, these soldiers may also have seen a need to defend their homes from their neighbors.

A combination of promises of local service with the threat of enforced service at last drew in enough volunteers to make up a brigade. According to W. Todd Groce, whose *Mountain Rebels: East Tennessee Confederates and the Civil War, 1860–1870,* is a valuable reference, enrolling officers were willing to give, perhaps sincerely, the needed assurances. Groce quotes one officer as stating flatly that volunteers joining him "will not be liable to be taken out of the state." Another recruiter was more careful: "The Regiment will be subject only to the orders of the General commanding the Department of East Tennessee and it is not likely that it will be ordered out of the Department."[4]

Since enactment of the Conscription Law of April 1862, forced service had been a possibility. However, the law had not been uniformly or rigidly applied. One would-be company commander reported that he "would fill my company in three days," if men feared that conscription was to be strictly enforced.[5]

By the end of September, enthusiastic recruiting, optimistic assurances of local duty, and the fear of a draft produced enough volunteers for a brigade. The official standard of the time called for one hundred men to a company and ten companies to a regiment. On September 27, 1862, three regiments were organized. These were the last volunteer units organized in East Tennessee. They were originally designated the Seventy-ninth, Eightieth, and Eighty-first Tennessee Regiments and later renamed the Sixtieth, Sixty-first, and Sixty-second. The newer numbering is used throughout this work, although the original designation sometimes appeared in official reports at least as late as April 1863.

On October 3, 1862, John C. Vaughn was promoted to brigadier general, to rank from September 22. The new brigade of approximately three thousand men was officially mustered in to the Confederate army on November 7. Vaughn was immediately ordered out of East Tennessee, beginning the long journey that took him to the assistance of Gen. John C. Pemberton in the defense of Vicksburg. Although this decision certainly disappointed the men who hoped to defend their home turf, it could not have been a surprise to anyone who knew the opinions of the Confederate leaders. The generals in charge did not trust their East Tennessee troops.

Gen. Samuel Jones was commander of the Department of East Tennessee when Vaughn was ordered out of the area, but the distrust of local loyalty was embedded in policy by his predecessor, Gen. E. Kirby Smith.

A native of Florida, Smith (or Kirby Smith, as he came to call himself to avoid confusion with other Smiths) resigned his commission in the U.S. Army when his home state seceded. All of his Confederate service had been in Virginia until he was transferred to command the Department of East Tennessee. Whether because of his brief experience with Vaughn's regiment at Bull Run, or for some other reason, Kirby Smith immediately demonstrated his lack of faith in the local troops now under his command.

Kirby Smith arrived in Knoxville on March 8, 1862. On March 13, 1862, he sent to Adj. Gen. Samuel Cooper in Richmond a report filled with doubt, writing, "It is not an individual opinion that some of the regiments from this region are disloyal, but it is the conviction of many of our friends . . . I cannot, therefore, too strongly urge upon the Department the propriety, if not the necessity, of removing these troops to some other point." On April 8, President Davis formally declared East Tennessee as enemy territory, suspending civil jurisdiction except in civil litigation and suspending the writ of habeas corpus.[6]

Kirby Smith's tenure in the department was brief. He served from March 8 to August 14, when Gen. John P. McCown succeeded him. McCown was replaced by Samuel Jones on September 19, who left about a month later, when Kirby Smith returned to the position. This rapid series of command changes was perhaps both a cause and a symptom of the Confederacy's uneasy hold on East Tennessee.

Jones may not have been as outspoken on the loyalty question as was Kirby Smith, but he adhered to the same policy. Following his orders, Vaughn and his new brigade boarded a train at Knoxville for their long trip to Vicksburg. While the western theater of operations undoubtedly required reinforcement, the decision to send this untrained brigade had more to do with prejudice than with strategy. Kirby Smith commented that "the advantage of this change was, it . . . transfers the East Tennessee, which, though good troops, are better away from the Union influences by which they are here surrounded."[7]

Upon arrival in Mississippi in December 1862, Vaughn moved to Grenada, where Gen. John C. Pemberton was prepared to fight the Union army commanded by Ulysses S. Grant. In July 1862, General Grant had been appointed to command the District of West Tennessee. On October 25, 1862, his command was elevated to departmental status. Shortly thereafter he began a two-pronged thrust into Mississippi, leading one part of his army due south along the Mississippi Central Railroad. Pemberton had confronted Grant, then withdrawn to Grenada, about 110 miles north of Jackson. Instead of advancing to challenge the Confederates, Grant was forced to withdraw to Memphis after Gen. Earl Van Dorn led a cavalry raid that destroyed the Union supply base at Holly Springs. The second prong of Grant's planned assault was a move down the river from Memphis led by Gen. William T. Sherman; this led to the battle of Chickasaw Bluffs at the end of December.

On December 23, Vaughn was ordered to move his brigade from Grenada to Vicksburg and was assigned by Pemberton to a position at the extreme left, or northern, end of the line of Vicksburg's defenses, where the obstacles to an attack, both natural and man-made, were very strong.

The brigade first heard hostile shots on December 28, 1862, when they marched from Vicksburg's hills down to face General Sherman's attack at Chickasaw Bayou. The Tennesseans' losses were small, because Union forces concentrated their efforts on less well-fortified parts of the line. In his report on the battle, Gen. Martin Luther Smith described Vaughn's position: "The formidable abatis in front of General Vaughn, together with the batteries in position in the line to his rear, seemed to have disheartened the enemy there from the first, rendering his attack uncertain, feeble, and easily repulsed."[8] The brigade reported eight men killed and ten wounded.

Nevertheless, Pemberton, apparently satisfied that what little was done, was done well, gave Vaughn a mild commendation, noting that he performed his duties "in an entirely satisfactory manner," and specifically mentioned among regiments "entitled to the highest distinction" the Eightieth [i.e., Sixty-first] Tennessee, which he described in his official report on the battle as behaving "with resolution and unflinching courage."[9]

Whatever Pemberton thought of the performance of Vaughn's men in December, he did not take them with him in May, when he moved out of Vicksburg's defenses to attack Grant. Pemberton's decision to march toward Grant illustrates the strategic dilemma he faced.

On December 19, President Jefferson Davis had arrived in Mississippi to review the defenses of Vicksburg and to discuss strategy with his senior commander in the west, Gen. Joseph E. Johnston. Davis, Johnston, and Pemberton met in Grenada on December 24. This was perhaps one of the most significant strategic conferences of the war. The president's first priority was the defense of Vicksburg. Johnston advocated instead the concentration of all available forces in his army in the field, even at the risk of leaving Vicksburg uncovered, in order to confront the Union army and force it to give battle. The differing views of Davis and Johnston were not reconciled. Throughout the ensuing campaign, Pemberton struggled unsuccessfully to serve both masters, with unfortunate results.[10]

As late as early May, Pemberton was faced with conflicting orders. On May 7, President Davis telegraphed him, "To hold both Vicksburg and Port Hudson is necessary." On May 13, General Johnston sent word from Jackson, "All the strength you can quickly assemble should be brought."[11] Pemberton's inability to overcome the burden of clashing strategies is best shown by his action before the battle of Champion Hill. He held a council of war with his senior commanders on May 14 and decided to march to join Johnston. But he did so with only half a heart, and only two-thirds of his army. Instead of concentrating his entire force, Generals Smith and Forney were left in Vicksburg, and General Vaughn at Big Black Bridge, with a total of approximately 11,000 men. The remaining 22,000 marched east toward Jackson.[12]

The climax of this movement was the battle of Champion Hill on May 16. Pemberton's defeat there sealed the fate of Vicksburg, as he was forced to fall back, and never again had as good a chance to join forces with Johnston to defeat the Federal army. Decisive as it turned out to be for Grant's Vicksburg campaign, Champion Hill may have had even broader significance. Edwin Bearss, author of the comprehensive *Campaign for Vicksburg,* believes it to have been the hinge on which the war turned, calling it "the most important single engagement in the Civil War."[13]

Before the battle of Champion Hill, Vaughn's brigade had been ordered out of Vicksburg to defend the railroad bridge over the Big Black River. (There was also a second, makeshift bridge below the rail crossing constructed by mooring a small steamboat across the river and planking over the deck.) At that point, about twelve miles from Vicksburg, the railroad running west from Jackson entered a horseshoe bend formed by the river, which flows west to the north of the tracks and roughly parallel to them, until it turns to the south, then back in an easterly direction. To the south of the tracks, between them and the returning river, was a tangled cypress brake known as Gin Lake.

The brake was impassable, so that the line of defense ran from the northern edge of Gin Lake across the tracks and continued north until it met the river, a distance of about a mile. The railroad bridge crossed this low area on trestles, rising gradually to the river and its western bank, which was fifty feet or so higher than the eastern side. A shallow bayou meandered north from the tracks to the river. Confederate engineers used the bayou as a moat and constructed a defensive line behind it, felling trees across it to form an abatis. This line north of the tracks was provided with little or no artillery. It was considered a strong position, with the bayou and abatis, and, in any case, dense woods about four hundred yards to the front obstructed the line of fire.

The East Tennessee troops were clearly insufficient to hold this line against Grant's army, but they were a precaution against a raiding detachment. When Pemberton began his retreat after Champion Hill, the Big Black position became vital to his plan, and the line was accordingly reinforced. Gen. John S. Bowen of Missouri was given command of the rearguard action. He placed a brigade of Missourians under Col. Francis M. Cockrell in the open land between the railroad and Gin Lake, supported by artillery. Immediately north of the tracks he positioned Vaughn's Sixtieth Tennessee. To their left was the Sixty-second, and to their left was the Sixty-first. Occupying the remainder of the line from Vaughn's position north to the river was Bowen's Second Brigade, commanded by Gen. Martin E. Green. In all, Bowen had about five thousand men with which to hold back the advancing Federal troops.

Pemberton has been criticized for trying to hold the Big Black line for as long as he did, but he had good reason. While all of the army that was with him, except for Bowen's rearguard, had crossed the river by the morning of May 17, Pemberton was waiting for the division led by Gen. William W. Loring. Loring and his 6,300 men had become separated from the main force after Champion Hill, and Pemberton expected this important division to rejoin him. He did not know that Loring had marched off in a southeasterly direction and was not attempting to return.

Early in the morning on May 17, the Federals attacked. On the Union right, the charge was led by Gen. Michael Lawler, a large, colorful Irishman whose favorite saying was, "If you see a head, hit it."[14] Lawler charged obliquely across the front of Green's position on the Confederate left and struck at Vaughn's Sixty-first regiment, approximately in the center of the Confederate line. Pemberton, across the river, watched Vaughn's troops abandon the prepared defenses at the first sight of the enemy and flee or surrender. Because of its position farther along the line away from the initial attack, John Earnest and the Sixtieth did not feel the full force of the first assault, but they nevertheless surrendered readily to the attackers in front of them. Their position next to the tracks allowed Earnest and a nimble few others to escape across the bridge.

Lawler later reported that his 1,200 prisoners were more men than he had brought into the battle. Total Confederate losses were approximately 200 killed or wounded and 1,751 captured. Union killed, wounded, and missing came to 279 men. As he watched the remnant of his rearguard straggle toward Vicksburg (at least the men paused long enough to burn the bridges, delaying Grant's pursuit), Pemberton remarked despairingly to an aide, "Just thirty years ago I began my military career . . . and today—the same date—that career has ended in disaster and disgrace."[15] In his formal report on the affair, dated August 25, 1863, he criticized General Vaughn's performance: "so strong was the position, that my greatest, almost only, apprehension was a flank movement [across the river at other points] which would have endangered my communications with Vicksburg. Yet this position was abandoned by our troops almost without a struggle and with the loss of nearly all of our artillery . . . Brigadier-General Vaughn's brigade had not been engaged at Baker's Creek; his men were fresh, and I believed were not demoralized . . . The troops occupying the center [Vaughn's] did not do their duty . . . I have received no report from Brigadier-General Vaughn of the operations of his brigade on this occasion."[16] So far as the record shows, he never did.

Although one of Vaughn's regimental commanders, Col. James G. Rose, writing years later, attempted to shift the blame, there is no doubt that the brigade behaved shamefully.[17] The real question is *why*. For those Confederates who had not trusted the East Tennesseans' loyalty from the beginning, this was their proof. However, there is little direct evidence in the diary either to support or rebut this accusation.

Relying solely on Earnest's indirect testimony, the answer is failure under fire due to lack of training and lack of leadership. The diary contains several examples of lax discipline. As for leadership, Colonel Rose, commander of the Sixty-first Regiment, writes in his history of the regiment of seeing the troops from Champion Hill retreat over the bridge and expecting at any moment to receive his own orders to withdraw.[18] Clearly he had no thought of being the steadfast rearguard that Pemberton expected.

No Confederate involved in the rout at the Big Black River won any glory. But at least a few, John Earnest and John Vaughn among them, proved that a lack of loyalty was not the problem, by staying with their cause and fighting on until April 1865. Those of Vaughn's command who made it back to Vicksburg were placed again behind the strong upper defenses and waited out the siege there.

When Pemberton retired behind the gates of Vicksburg after the defeat at Big Black River, he was in a defensive position of almost legendary strength. Shelby Foote, writing in *The Civil War,* gives an excellent view of the defenses:

> Skillfully constructed, well sited, and prepared for a year against the day of investment, the fortifications extended for seven miles along commanding ridges and were anchored at both extremities to the lip of the sheer 200-foot bluff, north and south of the beleaguered city. Forts, redoubts, salients, redans, lunets and bastions had been erected or dug at irregular intervals along the line, protected by overlapping fields of fire and connected by a complex of trenches, which were in turn mutually supporting. There simply was no easy way to get at the defenders.[19]

Grant brought his army to this fortress on May 18, the day after Big Black. He attacked immediately and was thrown back. On May 22, a second assault was also unsuccessful. Counting 4,141 Union casualties from the two attempts with no advance of position, Grant accepted the necessity of a siege.

There was continuing conflict over the following weeks, primarily artillery duels, sniping, and some attempts at mining the fortifications, but Grant was mainly content to hold his constrictive line, waiting for diminishing stores of supplies, especially food, to take their toll on the defenders.

On July 3, with his men down to quarter rations, and those of poor quality, Pemberton polled his senior commanders on the possibility of attempting to break through the surrounding Federals. There was no support for such an action. Gen. John H. Forney, for example, reported "the unanimous opinion of the brigade and regimental commanders that the physical condition and health of our men are not sufficiently good to enable them to accomplish successfully the evacuation."[20]

Whatever their condition, they were clearly outnumbered. By mid-June, Grant had assembled 71,000 troops at Vicksburg. They were placed in two lines, one facing Pemberton's feeble 29,000 in Vicksburg, the other guarding against the possibility of an attack by Johnston's 31,000 men hovering to their east, near Jackson. On July 3, Pemberton met Grant between the lines to discuss terms. On July 4, 1863, he surrendered Vicksburg.

When the Vicksburg garrison surrendered, General Grant agreed to parole the 29,000 Confederates. It was expected that in due course the paroled men would be declared exchanged and freed to fight again. However, a special arrangement was available for East Tennesseans. There was concern that loyal Unionists among the East Tennessee prisoners should not be forced back into Confederate service: "Andrew Johnson [military governor of Tennessee] also took steps to have Vicksburg prisoners enrolled in the Union army. Johnson, with the assistance of General William S. Rosecrans, urged the War Department to allow Rebel prisoners of war to join the Federal ranks. After considerable wavering, Washington finally consented."[21]

Embarrassed as a leader at the Big Black River, his surrendered troops welcomed into the well-fed Union army, little could have been expected of John Vaughn after Vicksburg. It may be that he accomplished little more. And yet he soldiered on, offering at least, a lesson in stubborn and dedicated loyalty.

Of the 2,700 men reported by Vaughn in December 1862, there remained 1,576 to be paroled by General Grant in July 1863. In anticipation of their exchange, the brigade was directed to assemble at Jonesboro, Tennessee. General Vaughn was exchanged July 13, 1863.[22]

By mid-October 1863, Vaughn had a brigade active in the field, reconstituted with troops from other units and whatever men from his old brigade were both exchanged and willing. The temptation of nearby homes proved too much for many men. Large numbers of Vaughn's former troops never reported for duty again.

As General Vaughn lamented to Jefferson Davis, "I am sorry to say that our Vicksburg prisoners in East Tennessee are not reporting for duty." He then requested that what men he could muster be turned into mounted infantry: "My opinion is that out of the seven regiments paroled at Vicksburg we will not get out of the enemy's lines more than three regiments, and they all would make a fine mounted command." (The seven regiments referred to encompass all of the East Tennessee troops who served at Vicksburg, not just the three regiments that had been under Vaughn's command.)[23]

The decision to mount Vaughn's troops was not universally approved. When he read of it, Gen. James Longstreet wrote on December 26, 1863, "I would respectfully suggest that we have already more cavalry than we need, and not enough infantry." Longstreet's opposition to additional cavalry was more general than a lack of confidence in Vaughn: "Partisan cavalry, having authority to keep and sell everything that they capture, do not always confine their captures to the enemy's side . . . The other cavalry seems to have taken up the idea that they should enjoy like privileges . . . I fear that this feeling to acquire property is more at heart with much of our cavalry than a disposition to drive the enemy from our soil."[24]

Vaughn's deficiencies as a commander should not be allowed to obscure his personal bravery. Col. G. G. Dibrell, reporting the result of an engagement on October 20, 1863, testified to Vaughn's courage: "Brigadier-General Vaughn had kindly volunteered his services, which were invaluable to me, and his gallantry and daring charge upon the enemy has endeared him to my brigade and caused them all to regard him as one of the bravest of the brave."[25]

A report of the forces in East Tennessee on December 31, 1863, lists four regiments in Vaughn's brigade, but not the Sixtieth, Sixty-first, and Sixty-second Tennessee; those three are collectively denominated "Second East Tennessee Brigade (detachment), Maj. James A. Rhea." Vaughn's entire command is reported as 998 officers and men, "aggregate present and absent."[26]

A May 6, 1864, report lists a total "aggregate present" in Vaughn's brigade of 1,938 officers and men, including "Detachments of Vaughn's old brigade, Sixtieth, Sixty-first, and Sixty-second Tennessee Regiments . . . 48." Those forty-eight men were all that remained of the brigade that arrived in Vicksburg in December 1862 with a total strength of 2,734.[27]

This report, transmitted to Gen. Braxton Bragg in Richmond by Lt. Col. Archer Anderson, assistant adjutant general, is particularly critical of General Vaughn: "General V. has no idea of discipline. Some of the commands are good; from what I can ascertain, the great fault is with the commander of the brigade. Another officer should be put in command of the mounted men, and General V. be made to take the dismounted and be assigned to some infantry division, under a strict officer."[28]

The lack of discipline in Vaughn's command may have been egregious but was hardly unique. In his memoir of service on the staff of Gen. John C. Breckinridge, J. Stoddard Johnston gave his impression of the cavalry in June 1864: "There were W. L. Jackson's brigade, McCausland's brigade, Vaughn's brigade, Imboden's brigade, and a number of smaller organization, the whole being about three thousand cavalry most of it known as wild cavalry—of the efficiency of which there was constant complaint and almost daily exhibition."[29]

At the battle of Piedmont, Virginia, on June 5, 1864, the Confederates were defeated and the general commanding, William E. "Grumble" Jones was killed. Jones had placed his infantry at the left of his line with the cavalry or mounted infantry to the right. There was a gap between the two placements. The Union attack against the infantry was fierce, and just as fiercely contested. Generals Vaughn and John D. Imboden, commanding the mounted troops on the right, observed the action but failed to join in. The result was that the Confederates suffered a defeat, with the loss of an able, if contentious, commander.

Vaughn, who was senior to Imboden, received the heaviest share of the blame for the failure to attack. It is now difficult to understand why the two generals sat astride their horses and watched the Federal attack on their infantry without taking part in the defense. Vaughn left no record of this action. Imboden in later years wrote two accounts that differ in material particulars.

One of the keys is the interpretation of an order from Jones to Vaughn and Imboden.

The historian who produced the most detailed account of the battle concluded: "From his two accounts it is evident that he [Imboden] considered Jones' order a strict prohibition of his engaging at discretion. Likewise, Vaughn's inaction may have stemmed from a similar interpretation of the order."[30] Nevertheless, it would seem that common sense, which has been known to break out occasionally even among the higher ranks of the military, would have spurred Vaughn and Imboden on to the aid of their fellow soldiers.

One of the more dramatic actions of the late war was Jubal Early's raid of June–July 1864, which brought Confederate troops, at least briefly, to the gates of Washington, D.C. Vaughn's brigade took part, but again not without controversy. As Early was moving to the valley to begin his march, Gen. John Breckinridge sent orders to Vaughn at 5:30 A.M. on July 16, 1864: "I am unable to take command today [Breckinridge was recovering from an injury] . . . Assume it . . . Confer with General D. H. Hill [the order also included specific directions about troop movements]."

At 10:30 A.M. on the same day, a member of Breckinridge's staff wrote to Vaughn: "General: The enclosed communication (copy) was sent to you at 5:30 A.M. General Hill has just informed the major-general commanding that the troops have not been placed in position, and the tenor of his note indicates that you have not conferred with him. He desires me to ascertain from you the reason which has prevented compliance with instructions so explicit, and the failure to observe which may involve such serious consequences."[31] In spite of criticism, Vaughn persevered. He was wounded in the ankle near Martinsburg on September 2, and after his recovery he returned to East Tennessee.[32]

In a dispatch dated September 7, 1864, Gen. John Echols, then commanding the Department of Western Virginia and East Tennessee, described his assignment in despairing terms: "The condition of East Tennessee is a very bad one, the large majority of the people being opposed in sentiment to us, and the country being filled with bushwhackers and marauders in organized bands . . . Some portions of Southwestern Virginia were also fast coming to the same condition."

After offering considerable detail supporting this description, Echols concludes, "I found Brigadier-General Vaughn in the department, and I have assigned him temporarily to the command of the troops in the field in East Tennessee, as I found that he had the confidence of the people there, and also the respect and confidence of the troops."[33]

The expression of support by General Echols undoubtedly cheered Vaughn, but even his stubborn spirit weakened at times. By February 13, 1865, he was writing plaintively to Echols,

> I have always done the best I could; tried to do right in all things. East Tennessee is filled up with a class of citizens that are hard to please, and the officer who commands in this department has or will have a hard time, especially here in East Tennessee. If you can supply my place I shall not object to being relieved from this department. To command troops who have not been paid for nineteen months, poorly clothed and armed, and then kept on the front all the time, fighting more or less, is no pleasant position.[34]

Vaughn wrote again to Echols on February 17, "I have just forwarded requisitions for all we needed. We need everything. My ordnance officers cannot get papers enough to make requisitions on; same condition at my headquarters." Nevertheless, he concludes this report,

> I am doing all I can for the good of the cause and service, and shall continue to do until this war closes, in some capacity; but as I am not a West Pointer, some one might do better in my place. . . but I am ready and willing to obey all orders. Whatever you think best, order me to do. My heart is in this death struggle of ours and I want to do my duty.[35]

Even when the struggle seemed to most men to be over, Vaughn could not accept the verdict. On April 12, at Christiansburg, Virginia,

Vaughn was with Echols when word came that Robert E. Lee had surrendered at Appomattox on April 9. Echols immediately disbanded his command. The war ended for John Earnest on that day.[36] But for John Vaughn, the struggle was to continue. He called for volunteers and got about four hundred men. He apparently intended to join General Johnston in North Carolina, but lack of supplies and rapid desertions from his small force defeated that plan. Vaughn then joined the dwindling band of loyalists accompanying Jefferson Davis and was one of the five brigade commanders who took part in the last council of war held by President Davis.[37]

On May 9, 1865, leaving his few troops in Washington, Georgia, General Vaughn met in nearby Augusta with Union General Emory Upton to negotiate terms of surrender. He won permission for his men to retain their horses.[38]

Defeated at last, Vaughn returned to the world of commerce. For a time he tried his hand at business in New York City, where his first wife died in 1869. He returned to Tennessee. Although he must have faced some of the hostility that still divided people in the region, he was nevertheless popular enough to win election to one term in the Tennessee State Senate. Vaughn then moved farther south, to the plantation of his second wife's family in Brooks County, near Thomasville, Georgia. He died there on September 10, 1875.[39]

PART II

The Diary of
John Guilford Earnest

I

From East Tennessee
to Vicksburg

Determined today to keep a diary in order that my habits may be made the more regular and that I may have a synopsis of the most striking occurrences for reference.

Arose this morning at reveille—was greeted by calls for beef—put the men off expecting some soon—didn't make a raise until late in the evening. Went up to Company B and had a nice game of euchre.

At half past eight retired. Very tired. Weather fine.

The regiment was stationed at Brush Creek Camp, Haynesville, Tennessee.

SATURDAY, OCTOBER 25TH

Arose late this morning, found it had been raining during the night and was still at it. Continued to rain until about ten o'clock when it turned to sleet and was soon snowing. By three o'clock the ground was covered and still falling.

Concluded it would be good policy to go out for the night and escape the cold and danger from falling timber. Went accordingly out to Mr. Young's in company with George McNabb. Had quite a nice time though considerably crowded. Retired early to a very comfortable bed.

MONDAY, OCTOBER 27TH

Arose at the usual hour. Issued and every thing went on as usual.

At 12 o'clock midnight started to Knoxville. Had quite a time. The train so crowded with sick and wounded that a seat was not to be had. After arriving at Jonesboro, I went to the mail car and by a little begging got a place by the stove. The train being behind time we ran by the breakfast house at Mossy Creek hungry.

Arrived at Knoxville about ten A.M. Found a large portion of Bragg's army there so that no breakfast was to be procured.

Went to work to try for my commissary stores—found the officers at the department quite a high headed set. After waiting and watching all day succeeded in drawing sugar, rice and salt.

Had to pay a dollar and run a foot race for my dinner at the Tennessee Hotel. Got supper at a private boarding house—not much. Met up with my old friend Jaycock. He is a lieutenant in the 14th Tennessee Regiment.

Finding quarters but poor and chances slim in town I determined to walk out to McMillan, as the boys had gone ahead. Got very tired of my bargain before I got there, and the pleasure of sleeping in a wood shed after I arrived—"no rest for the wicked."

Gen. Braxton Bragg assumed command of the Army of Tennessee on June 27, 1862. McMillan was six or seven miles outside of Knoxville, back up the rail route that Earnest had just traveled.

TUESDAY, OCTOBER 28TH

Left McMillan this morning at five A.M. Passed along very smoothly, forming the acquaintance of Esq. Armstrong of Rogersville.

Arrived at Fullens at four A.M. Stayed over until the train came at nine A.M. found all well. Arrived at camp Crawford on time with a very bad cold.

The Earnest home was in Fullens, now Chuckey.

WEDNESDAY, OCTOBER 29TH

Nothing of importance. Everything working as usual.

THURSDAY, OCTOBER 30TH

Nothing of unusual importance. Rode to the country in the evening and succeeded in getting some beef for the boys. Went up to Capt. Gammon's quarters and had a game of euchre. Retired early not feeling very well.[1]

FRIDAY, OCTOBER 31ST

Have got all right again. Nothing of importance occurring.

TUESDAY, NOVEMBER 18TH

After finding a moment's leisure I determined to write up my long neglected diary.

Was very busily engaged all day getting up rations to start to Sweetwater. The boys all seem very anxious to go and I feel a little of the same anxiety myself, but still keep thinking all the while that I may be as anxious to return.

Retired very tired tonight.

On November 3, 1862, the Sixtieth Regiment was inspected by Maj. T. W. W. Davies, acting inspector general, Department of East Tennessee. He reported, "This regiment is composed of good men, tolerably well clothed. Supplied with camp and garrison equipage, but without arms and accoutrements."[2] There is no record of when the men were issued weapons.

Armed or not, the newly organized East Tennesseans had been ordered to Mobile, and, as it turned out, on to the defense of Vicksburg. Sweetwater, the home of General Vaughn, was about forty miles down the railroad line south of Knoxville. The destination of the brigade turned out to be Knoxville, a more logical location for staging a major transfer.

WEDNESDAY, NOVEMBER 19TH

At four o'clock this morning the drum beat reveille and the order went forth to strike tents. We ate a hurried snack and in forty minutes all the encampment was leveled and the tents rolled ready for traveling. Soon we were on the road loaded. After considerable bustling everything was ready—the engineer whistled off the rubbers and we moved slowly away. As we rolled by Camp Crawford a farewell shout rent the air and we all bid adieu to her crystal streams and beautiful groves. Strange feelings rushed upon me as we were passing. I had learned to love the situation and had accustomed myself to feel at home amid her bowers so that as I thought perhaps I may never again behold this scene—how many is there among us who will ever again live to visit our old camping ground?—and other thoughts which I cannot now describe. A thrill—a feeling of regret, sorrow and gladness mingled stole over me.[3]

Soon the spell was broken by our arrival at Jonesboro where the ladies it was reported would be out to see us pass—with numerous delicacies and for some a smile perhaps a *tear*. I had placed myself in the door in order to improve the moments as much as possible, but to my great indignation the engineer *ran by* without even checking up.

I didn't recover my temper until I got to Fullens where I met the home folks with some *things* for me. (I say *things* because I don't care to be *definite* now). The trip was very pleasant, the boys being hoarse from exercising their lungs too freely long before we reached Knoxville—which we did (i.e. reached K.) about ten A.M.

Thursday, November 20th (Knoxville)

We remained in the cars until twelve o'clock today when we moved out to camp and christened it Camp Vaughn. Occupied the day in fixing up our tents etc.

Retired early having slept but little the evening before.

Friday, November 20th

Nothing of interest occurred today.[4]

Saturday, November 22nd

Visited the city this morning and drew rations, etc. Met up with Tim Henderson who came out to camp with me. Nothing of interest.

Sunday, November 23rd

Arose this morning and received orders to draw rations to move on Tuesday, drew them and ran around town a little. Nothing of interest further except a visit to Latrobes Battery.[5]

Monday, November 24th

Nothing of interest today.

Tuesday, November 25th

This morning we struck tents to leave Knoxville for Mobile, Ala. Left Knoxville at eight A.M. and arrived at Dalton, Ga. eight A.M. and raining.

After ascertaining that we were to stay all night, Tate, Will Rankin and I struck for Cousin Nick Earnest's. Found the folks generally well, and had a most hearty reception. Was introduced to Cousins Ella and Mattie Waugh. After having spent a very pleasant time having some music etc. we retired.[6]

> *In 1862, the rail line from Knoxville through Sweetwater and Cleveland to Dalton was probably somewhere between 100 and 110 miles. At an apparent average speed of 9 miles per hour or less, the twelve-hour trip seems to have been rather a leisurely journey. Robert Black, in his authoritative treatment of the railroads of the time, says that "the average southern train of the sixties seldom exceeded a speed of 25 miles per hour." It appears doubtful that John Earnest's train ever attained that speed.[7]*
>
> *One of the most interesting features of this diary here and in later entries is its illustration of the deficiencies of Confederate rail transportation.*

WEDNESDAY, NOVEMBER 26TH

Arose this morning at five, found the balance of the family astir and a comfortable fire in the parlor. After eating a hearty breakfast we all bid the "gude folk" good-by and were soon off for Atlanta, which latter place we reached about four o'clock A.M. Only stayed here about two hours when we left for West Point.

THURSDAY, NOVEMBER 27TH (WEST POINT)

After riding all night up to three o'clock this morning we drew up at this little town. The boys were all out by the time we were stopped in search of brandy, which they found plenty, and of course the regiment all got drunk but a few. Major Rhea stationed guards at all the groceries but in spite of guards and everything else the boys succeeded in getting a bountiful supply.[8]

Remained at West Point until 10 A.M. when we left for Montgomery which place we reached about 10 P.M.

In John Jackman's diary of his service in the First Kentucky Brigade, he preserves the record of his own trip from West Point to Montgomery on May 28, 1863: "The regiment left at 10 A.M. on a train of flat cars. Dr. B. and I, with a barrel of whisky in charge (Jackman's emphasis), left at 1 A.M., on passenger train. Rain commenced pouring down about 11 A.M. and continued until next morning. Our train passed the regiment just before we got to Montgomery, and the boys looked like drowned rats. At the depot, the whiskey was issued out by buckets-full."[9]

Excessive drinking was, unfortunately, prevalent in the Confederate army. Bell I. Wiley, in his classic THE LIFE OF JOHNNY REB, *points out that the concern was so great that "the War Department issued a general order early in 1862 entreating commanders of all grades to suppress drunkenness by every means in their power."[10]*

If one is shocked at the East Tennesseans being drunk before ten o'clock in the morning, one must at least admire their initiative. They had to forage on their own, unlike the better organized Kentuckians, who had their whiskey provided for them.

FRIDAY, NOVEMBER 28TH (MONTGOMERY, ALA.)

After sitting in the car all night I was glad to see daylight come, at which time I began to look around for my whereabouts and found we were in a low flat country in sight of the city.

At ten o'clock we moved off from the road to our camping grounds and went into camp—as we found orders for us on our arrival, directing us to await further orders at this place. In the evening we walked over to town and found it to be quite a nice place although we could see but little of it, being only a short distance in town.

On December 1, Gen. John H. Forney, Commander, District of the Gulf, wrote from his headquarters in Mobile to Gen. John C. Pemberton in Mississippi: "I am directed by General Bragg so soon as the Tennessee regiments (Brigadier-General Vaughn's command) arrive to send a strong brigade of infantry to Meridian subject to your orders, but to be recalled whenever we are threatened here. I have directed General Vaughn to proceed, without stopping, to Meridian with his command, agreeably to these instructions."[11]

Vaughn's men arrived in Montgomery on November 27 and did not leave until December 2. The delay was clearly related to the expectation of new orders mentioned in this entry, but in any case the inadequate transportation system would have prevented a swift passage through the city. The Montgomery and West Point Railroad used 4' 8½" gauge track. The Alabama & Florida Railroad of Alabama, running from Montgomery to Pollard, across the bay from Mobile, used 5' gauge track. Further complicating matters, the Montgomery depots of the two roads were on opposite sides of the town, about a mile and a half apart. The movement of just one regiment from one depot to the other could take five hours. In December 1861, the Alabama Legislature had granted the Alabama & Florida permission to extend its line to the Montgomery and West Point depot. It was estimated that this would reduce the transfer time for one regiment to one hour. The connecting track was completed in September 1863.[12]

SATURDAY, NOVEMBER 29TH

This morning as soon as we got through with breakfast, Tate, George McNabb and I went over in a splendid carriage to town with a couple of sick men sent to the hospital. When we reached the hospital we deposited our sick and found on looking around that they were in the best of quarters, the hospital being neat and clean and furnished with first class surgeons. Here we found the "sisters of charity" busy in doing good. They seem to give every attention to the sick and to be eager to [*unintelligible*] the sufferings of others. Our horses being extremely gay the driver proposed to "*cool them off*" by driving us around town awhile—which offer we closed in with. Had quite a nice drive—Montgomery has some gay looking residences with beautiful arranged yards. The houses are generally made of wood and of spotless white while the grounds in front are shaded with arborvitae, orange and various evergreen trees frequently relieved by a clambering vine or bunch of cactus.

The ladies of Montgomery are not so beautiful as our East Tennessee mountain girls or the bonnie belles of Georgia, but still they possess a kind of languishing charm all their own.

At one o'clock we returned to camp and wrote a line to Pa. In the evening walked around a little visiting the gunboat in progress here and by the time we returned it was night. Retired early being very tired.

Earnest undoubtedly refers to the complex consisting of the General Hospital and the Ladies Hospital, located diagonally across from each other at the intersection of Bibb and Commerce Streets. Administration of the two institutions had been combined, under the name General and Ladies Hospitals.[13]

Another Confederate visiting Montgomery in 1862, Lt. Joe T. Scott, described the hospital as "very capacious and a well kept and well cared for institution," consisting of four brick buildings "fully sufficient to accommodate without crowding, one thousand patients." Six Sisters of Mercy from Mobile led the staff.[14]

It has not been possible to locate independent confirmation of Earnest's opinion of the relative beauty of the ladies of Montgomery.

SUNDAY, NOVEMBER 30TH

Spent the day in getting up rations. In the evening Dr. Harris preached to us a very interesting little war sermon. Being tired, I retired early.[15]

MONDAY, DECEMBER 1ST

Visited the city in the forepart of the day. In the evening we marched over to the Depot so as to be for moving to Mobile early in the morning.

Capt. Morrow and I finding the quarters for sleeping very uncomfortable, visited the theatre, returned late at night. Then threw myself down on an old tent and slept very comfortably.[16]

TUESDAY, DECEMBER 2ND

Everyone was astir by daylight getting things in order for leaving. At eight o'clock all were on board the train and we started on again. The country along our route was nothing more than medium, being generally low and swampy.

At Greenville, Ala. our train was delayed an hour and a half or two hours waiting for another train to pass. Tate and I strolled off to a house in search of an adventure. Walked in—was met at the door by a servant—called for some water which was brought to us in nice goblets and to my great horror when I threw out the water from my glass, the goblet and all went together. I offered to pay for the ware but was promptly refused the privilege by a smart lad of fourteen. I learned afterward that it was Mr. Merrell's goblet I had broken.

Not being satisfied with this experience we walked on up in town. By chance we formed the acquaintance of Capt. A. F. Posey, one of grandpa Earnest's old boarders. Were taken up to his brother in laws and introduced to his very interesting nieces, Misses Dora and Flora Herbert. On leaving we were presented with two splendid bouquets—here for the first time we saw the white japonica—a most splendid flower of large size.[17]

WEDNESDAY, DECEMBER 3RD

Arrived at Mobile Bay this morning at one o'clock. By four o'clock we were on board the steamer "Planter," a first-class passenger boat, and steaming away for the city twenty two miles off. After steaming around for some time in a big fog—we at length arrived at the wharf just as day was breaking.[18]

The boys were all moved out to some large warehouses out of the rain. I spent the greater portion of the day in running around in the rain getting up rations to move on.

By the way I called as soon as landing and got a first rate dish of oyster soup for breakfast—the same for dinner and supper. Felt very much like staying at this place as it gave promise of plenty to eat and a chance to see something.

Left Mobile late in the evening for Jackson, Miss. or rather directly for Meridian.

Thursday, December 4th (Meridian, Miss.)

Arrived at this place this morning at six o'clock in the midst of a tremendous rain.

After lying here some time the boys found out that it would be several hours before they could leave so they began to stir around for something to eat—having thrown their beef overboard on account of its being spoiled. I took a convenient seat and watched their movements. In a short time they found some cars laden with sugar and rice which they helped themselves to freely, every man filling his haversack and some even flour sacks. A few went so far as to carry off tobacco by the box—these I marked for future reference for I know they would steal at home—but am happy to state that I saw none of Company K engaged in this latter movement.

The day was a dreary one and the night none the less so. By hard work I secured a bed and retired early—but was drawn out before ten o'clock by the report that the regiment was ready to leave, but, finding that a portion would be left I stayed behind to make a draw of bacon.

Friday, December 5th (Meridian)

After spending a restless day—we at length got off for Jackson at 5 o'clock.

SATURDAY, DECEMBER 6TH (JACKSON, MISS.)

We arrived at this place this morning at four o'clock. Found some of the boys encamped by the road side and crawled in for a nap. Slept for a couple of hours and got up just at sunrise. Took some breakfast and then commenced to get every thing moved out to the balance of the regiment which was encamped about two miles from the city—succeeded in finding them without much trouble. Went to work and fixed things up—being tired went to bed early.

SUNDAY, DECEMBER 7TH

Visited the city today and found it like other cities of the times, crowded with soldiers and officers. The government officials in the commissary department seem to be quite a genteel set and very attentive to business. The town looks to be near the size of Knoxville perhaps a little larger.[19]

MONDAY, DECEMBER 8TH

Nothing of interest occurred from this date—except perhaps smallpox excitement, etc.—until the sixteenth of Dec. when we were ordered to cook rations for moving to Grenada, at which place the enemy had made their appearance.

WEDNESDAY, DECEMBER 17TH

We were all astir by daylight this morning and making preparations for getting off. By ten o'clock the regiment was on board the cars but did not get started until after eleven. Found a portion of the country through which we passed very fine while the balance was only medium.

At Canton, the Terminus of the N.O.J. & Great Northern R.R., we were delayed for some time and got out and looked around for a while—got some goober peas and cider at very high prices.[20]

Arrived at Grenada late at night and remained in the cars until daylight when we moved out to the country in a big pine wood and erected some huts for we had no tents. Made quite comfortable quarters.[21]

Thursday, December 18th (Grenada)

Occupied the time today principally in fixing things up and getting rations, also visited the fortifications. The place seems to be pretty well fortified, is naturally very strong. The place seems to be about played out as far as getting anything to eat or wear is concerned.

Pemberton's army was on the south bank of the Yalobusha River, protecting the railroad crossing at Grenada.

Friday, December 19th

The fore part of the day was spent in drawing etc. In the afternoon we were out on division review—being very anxious to see the sight I took position in a little peach tree about five feet off of the ground—by chance I fell in at the very place where the generals were posted for the review.

Gen. Price was the principal attraction. I got a full view of him. He is rather corpulent, about five feet ten inches tall and inclined to be corpulent. His face is one of the finest I ever saw. Hair nearly white, military whiskers of same color—perhaps not so gray by a shade. Rides a splendid black stallion with a white face.

Gen. Loring and Maj. Gen. Maurey were also present. Loring with his one arm presents quite a fine appearance—tall, square built, with a fine eye and heavy brown moustache, Gen. Maury is a small man with light hair and wears moustache and goatee—a la Louis Napoleon.

Sterling Price was a corps commander under Pemberton. Generals William W. Loring and D. H. Maury were division commanders.

SATURDAY, DECEMBER 20TH

At eight o'clock this morning the report came that the Yankees were advancing. In about an hour we were ordered to shoulder our muskets and cartridge boxes and march. The boys all did so without any hesitation. We posted on the Yallabusa in the rifle pits. After remaining there for some time we were ordered back to our fires as the alarm had proven to be false.

SUNDAY, DECEMBER 21ST

Nothing of interest occurred today outside of the usual monotony. Old Arab preached, I was up to hear him—put up a pretty good thing.

MONDAY, DECEMBER 22ND

The day was occupied principally in drawing rations. Whilst in town I met my old Emory friend, J. W. Ragsdale of Texas. He is now in the 24th Miss. Regt. with rank of 2nd Lieut. He came over to camp (rather to the woods) with me and spent a few hours— looks just the same old John.

TUESDAY, DECEMBER 23RD

Today we drew rations early and the boys were ordered to cook them and be in readiness to march by two o'clock. The hour arrived and we were moved out to the depot where we remained until some hours after dark—when our train was assigned to us and the boys boarded without further ceremony. I was fortunate enough to get a good bed and slept very soundly.[22]

WEDNESDAY, DECEMBER 24TH, 1862

Awoke this morning and found the cars just leaving for Jackson. Had an opportunity of seeing the country which we had passed in the night coming up. The land is low and very level, inclined to be swampy but very productive.

The weather was a little inclined to be "drippy" in the early portion of the day but cleared up toward evening.

When we got to Jackson we received the intelligence that heavy firing had been heard in the direction of Vicksburg. After remaining some time at the depot we got our tents on board and by dusk were off for the "Gibraltar of the West." Being Christmas Eve the boys were sending up rockets all along the road and everything seemed in unusually good spirits.

Slept but little during our run. That little was done in the latter portion of the night so that when I awoke at four A.M., I found myself in Vicksburg.

General Vaughn reported on operations December 26–29, 1862, without mentioning his arrival date; we may infer from that silence that he had arrived earlier than December 26. However, in his report covering the same events, General Pemberton is quite specific: "During the evening and night of this day (Pemberton is reporting activity for December 27) Brigadier Generals Vaughn and Gregg, with their brigades, arrived from Grenada . . . Before daylight they were moved to the front." It is clear from this diary entry that at least some of Vaughn's troops were in Vicksburg two days earlier than Pemberton states.[23]

Thursday, Christmas, December 25th

The first thing after getting out of the cars, I stumbled around until I found myself on the banks of "The Father of Waters." After taking a wash and getting my eyes fairly opened I began to look around. I had heard so much about the great Mississippi that I felt a thrill of satisfaction as I gazed upon her broad waters.

I spent a good portion of the day in looking around the city. Built on a rugged hillside sloping down to the water's edge, the houses look old and dusky, with an occasional old tower reared on some rugged steep that stands up far above those below. Her wharf once swarming with splendid steamers can now boast of but two or three old hulls of medium size. The streets everywhere are thronged with the military with nothing to remind one of the balmy old days gone by.

I stopped at the Washington Hotel, the only one of any character in the place—which seemed very strange to me for such a city as Vicksburg. My breakfast was a miserable affair—nothing but corn bread and beef with Rye coffee.

About two o'clock I started to camp—found one of Company A's men on the streets drunk and in a fair way to go to the guard house, so through kindness to him I went to him and prevailed upon him to go with me to camp—had quite a time with him. When I got to where the other boys were I was very tired and weak—nearly given out.

By the time we got our tents up and fixed for sleeping it was dark so we all put in early being very sleepy.

Vicksburg was built on a bluff overlooking a great hairpin bend in the Mississippi River, about two hundred feet below. Cannon on the bluff were sited so as to control traffic on the river, and the hills on which the city was built formed a naturally strong defensive position.

In addition to this significant military position, Vicksburg was an economic crossroads. The city long had been an important stopping place for river boatmen. By 1863, it was also a rail terminus. The Southern Railroad of Mississippi ran east to Jackson and there connected to roads running north into Tennessee, south to Mobile and New Orleans, and east into Alabama. Across the river to the west, the Vicksburg, Shreveport, and Texas Railroad brought goods from Louisiana and Texas for transshipment to the east. Despite its grand name, however, the line had been constructed only so far as Monroe, Louisiana, not to Texas, or even Shreveport.

Economic prosperity had brought considerable growth to Vicksburg. Reporting a population of 4,591 in the 1860 Census, Vicksburg was second in size in Mississippi to Natchez. Perhaps a third of the 3,100 white inhabitants were foreign born, and that cultural diversity undoubtedly added to the city's charm. From rowdy, even dangerous, saloons down by the river to the orchestra and repertory theater higher up on the bluff in the city proper, there was something for everyone. And there were three daily newspapers to report on all of the happenings. At least three hotels, of which the Washington was the finest, catered to the visiting gentry and tradesmen.

Vicksburg, then, was a vital link to the Confederate states west of the Mississippi, as well as a key point of control over river traffic. For both reasons, Jefferson Davis, whose own plantation was nearby, had insisted that the city should be held against Federal assault.[24]

Friday, December 26th (Vicksburg, Miss.)

The day was spent in getting up rations, etc. The Yankees continue to shell the woods on the Yazoo and are said to be landing some of their troops. The boys were all ordered into the trenches late this evening, but I did not go as I saw no prospect of a fight earlier than the next day.

General Sherman landed his men on the south bank of the Yazoo River, above Vicksburg, on December 26. They immediately moved south to the city's outer defenses at Chickasaw Bluffs. Vaughn's brigade was one of those in the Vicksburg defenses closest to this movement, posted as it was on the high bluffs at the left, or northern end, of the defensive line, not far from Fort Hill.

Saturday, December 27th

Arose early this morning much refreshed by a good sleep. The Regiment came in from the trenches about ten o'clock today. Late in the evening, Company K and Company I were ordered to picket the outposts. I remained in camp all night.

Sunday, December 28th

I was awakened this morning about four o'clock by heavy firing on our right. As soon as I eat a little breakfast after daylight I shouldered a musket and put out to join the boys in the swamps.

On arriving I found the firing to be still to their right by a few hundred yards.

It was the first time I ever heard the roar of a real battle which of course excited very peculiar feelings. We were looking every moment for them to make their appearance along our front. The firing for a time was very heavy—the muskets kept up a continual cracking, the light artillery was one continual roar while far in the distance could be heard at regular intervals the sound of the heavy guns from the enemy's fleet and Sniders bluff—reminding one of the heavy rolls of the base drum marking time for the smaller ones.

As our line was on the bank of Chickasaw Bayou, about ten o'clock Capt. Wash and myself concluded to stroll along the bank nearer to the engagement and take a view of what was going on and the scenery around us. We had got about two hundred yards from the rest of the command and seated ourselves on a log— quietly discussing the prospect ahead, when we were brought to our senses by the crack of half a dozen muskets from the other bank about two hundred yards below us—while the balls whistled harmlessly over our heads, one striking the water just in front of us.[25]

About 12 noon we were startled by the report of musketry from our post on the left, commanded by Lt. Bowling.[26] We soon found that the enemy were attempting to cut us off by flanking us on the left. We accordingly fell back a little way, posting the main body in line behind some large logs, while our watch extended obliquely backward on each wing. Here we awaited the enemy, but they failed to come any further.

About three o'clock in the afternoon the enemy moved up a battery near the position we had occupied in the morning and opened on our regiment over our heads. At the same time, Capt. Lynch replying with two twenty four pound Parrot guns. Also another small battery—which I did not know—posted in the hollow opposite our position opened. They soon silenced the Federal guns but not until they had killed two of our men and mortally wounded three more.[27]

At dark we were relieved, the company sleeping on their arms in the edge of the timber.

Monday, December 29th

The fight was carried on today at intervals, raging furiously a portion of the time on our right. Owing to the circumstance of this being the regular day for issuing rations I did not go out to the field. Our regiment while marching to the support of the 31st Tennessee came suddenly under a most galling fire from artillery, but fortunately we had but one man killed (who did not die immediately but properly speaking was mortally wounded).

By the 28th the Federals were in place and the next morning launched a determined, bloody, and unsuccessful attack against strong Confederate positions.

In repelling the Union assault, the Confederates suffered about 200 casualties, while the attackers reported their losses at the historically resonant number of 1,776. It was the failure of this thrust that convinced Grant that Vicksburg could be captured only if he could get below the city and come at it from the south and east.

In this, their first battle, Vaughn's brigade was at the extreme left of the line. There, the defenses were so strongly constructed that a successful attack was improbable. The brigade reported losses of eight killed and ten wounded.

Tuesday, December 30th

The day was passed in getting up rations etc. The enemy seem to be maneuvering as no fighting of consequence has occurred today.

Wednesday, December 31st

Everything quiet with the exception of occasional skirmishing today.

2

Waiting in the Trenches

Thursday, January 1st, 1863

We may now pause on the brink of the new year and steady ourselves for a peep into the last year and the prospect of the new one.

When we turn to the past all is dark; the blood of patriots and vandals mingle on a hundred battle fields from Donelson to Shiloah from Shiloah to Vicksburg. But though the best blood of the land has been poured out and the sigh of the mourner has been heard in every house—the hopes of thousands blighted—still the infernal hordes call for more blood—their fiendish appetites are still insatiate, though the accomplishment of their object is now grown into despair. Yet, with no other object than vengeance upon an unoffending people [they] rush on to desolate more hearthstones and make more lonely hearts.

But, thanks to the God of battles! They have seen their own hopes decay and their own hopes wither. Success has followed us on almost every side and we now begin to look to the day when the olive branch shall reign and war be spoken of as something in the past.

The day passed off with the usual monotonous camp duties. Nothing marked the entrance of the new year more than any other day—a circumstance which never happened to me before.

FRIDAY, JANUARY 2ND, 1863

The event which marked this day most in this vicinity was the retiring of the enemy. Their boats (or rather the smoke from them) can be distinctly seen going up the Mississippi, the Yazoo being clear of them entirely.

SATURDAY, JANUARY 3RD

Nothing of very particular interest occurred today.

SUNDAY, JANUARY 4TH

Nothing of interest. Dr. Pitts preached.[1]

SUNDAY, JANUARY 11TH

Briant Stephens was up to see me today. I was glad to see him. We spent the day very pleasantly together talking over our old scrapes, etc. In the evening we listened to a very good war talk from Col. Pitts.[2]

MONDAY, JANUARY 12TH

Tate suggested a trip to Jackson this morning. I accordingly got up my papers in the shape of a detail to get soap for the regiment, etc. Succeeded in getting them signed without much difficulty.

By half past eleven A.M. we were in the city all right for starting. After knocking around a little and taking a peach pye or two with spruce beer, we walked over to the Depot. Found the cars about ready to start and accordingly set about getting a seat. In the act of climbing up the car steps I recognized immediately before me my old acquaintance (of Emory notoriety) Sidney T. Frazer, now a 2nd Lieut. in a Georgia Regiment.

About ten miles above Vicksburg I saw a most beautiful lady—the first one I had seen in many a day. It was quite a treat though the train was running so fast that it was only a momentary enjoyment. My first impulse on beholding her was to *draw my cap,* which was immediately executed, and to my great delight she returned the salute with a graceful wave of the hand—and I *believe* her handkerchief with it, but *that hand* was so delicately turned that I could see nothing else for gazing at it.

We arrived at Jackson about five o'clock in the evening. Took supper at the Confederate House, and quite a hearty one at that, as it was the best I had seen in a long while—we even had *pure coffee,* very well made.

While supping we made our acquaintance with Adjt. Stark of 15th Miss Regiment. After we were through we went with him up to the Bowman House and engaged a room after some difficulty, the hotels all being very much crowded. The Adjutant having a bottle of good whiskey and appearing to be quite a nice fellow we all took a drink for the sake of luck.

There was a serenade on hand that night complimentary to General Price, who was stopping at the Confederate House. We went down with the crowd and got a position by the side of the old Hero. When called upon he arose and made a few remarks acknowledging the compliment, etc. He can't speak anything like he fights.

With an 1860 population of 3,191, Jackson was hardly a rival to the more prosperous cities on the river, but its position as both a rail crossing and the capital of the state supported several hotels. The Bowman was perhaps the finest. When General Grant entered the city on May 14, he stayed there, taking the same room that his opponent General Johnston had occupied the night before.[3]

TUESDAY, JANUARY 13TH (JACKSON)

After dreaming all night of fairy forms and fairy hands salut-
ing me by the roadside and other things which "no mortal e'er
dared dream before," I awoke and found myself on the fourth story
of the Bowman House and a cloudy sky outside.

Tate and I determined to get our concerns arranged as soon as
possible, but finding it would be several days before his could be
finished we put in our requisitions and started in a hack for Mrs.
Cade's, four miles in the country, where Tate was acquainted.

As we went along, notwithstanding the heavy rain that was
falling we succeeded in getting Misses Sallie and [Earnest's omis-
sion] Hardy and Mr. G. F. Hardy to go with us. We all soon drew
reins at Mrs. C's, and were duly welcomed, Tate seeming to be *one of
the family.* To my great surprise, I met "*Uncle Sam*"—(Lt. Dowthet
of Col. Rowan's Regt.) whose true name I never had known until
now. (I must mention here that Sergt.-Major Brown was with us we
having fallen in with him at Jackson).

That which attracts one most at the Widow's is a couple of
bonnie little lasses Misses Ann and Cynthia. Mr. Will Cade, the only
son grown, seems quite a clever young fellow.[4]

We passed the evening quite pleasantly by a large fire until
about half past eight when we were called into the dining room and
helped ourselves without any scruples to a splendid supper. After
supper we amused ourselves in various ways. The young ladies
were quite gay and Will Hardy proved quite a wit.

We retired about eleven o'clock and Tate and I plunged ourselves into a big feather bed "and thought we were in Heaven." I
feel certain that Miss Cynthia's auburn curls will be dangling about
me or the quiet smile of Miss Ann lighten my dreams.

WEDNESDAY, JANUARY 14TH

Arose this morning and found it still raining and accordingly
concluded to stay, as all parties seemed satisfied and the ladies

insisted that we shouldn't *think* of stirring on such a dreadful morning. The day passed off very pleasantly—in fact we had a real nice time—drinking beer and sitting around a huge parlor fire chatting with the ladies while the rain poured down in torrents outdoors.

Toward night it commenced snowing a little, so that we were confined indoors all day. But I felt no disposition to wander forth from so much good company and so much good eating, for our generous hostess certainly fed us like fighting cocks. The night was passed in a nearly similar manner to the one previous. We left a light snow on the ground when we retired which was late at night. Brown left for town this evening.

THURSDAY, JANUARY 15TH.

When I got up I found that a snow of about three inches depth had fallen. After taking a smoking breakfast of biscuit, squirrel, eggs & coffee, we warmed up a little and bid our kind friends adieu.

The road to town was rather disagreeable but we got there without much difficulty. On our arrival we found our business all right but no train leaving until next morning at nine o'clock. We spent the morning and a good portion of the afternoon loafing around the city with our old friend the Adjt. and Dr. Hobson, whose acquaintance we had formed before we went to the country.

About three o'clock I proposed to Tate that we go out to the Pearl River and see my old chum George C. Leavel. After a short discussion we determined to do so as chances in town were dull. The bridge having fallen in a day or two before, across the river we had to take passage by *Shank's express* and walk the railroad bridge.

At sundown we stopped at a little town of Negro cabins surrounded by a Leavel farm, with a small house out from the balance, and inquired the road to Mrs. Leavel's. An old darkey showed us in, informing us that "this am the place, right here." Having called for George we were shown to his room off to itself and he immediately made his appearance, recognizing me at once and seemed heartily glad to meet me. This reception was very gratifying to me after having been separated from my highly respected school fellow for so long a period.

At the supper table we were introduced to his sister, Miss *Tillie,* a—seemingly—very clever young lady—intelligent, good looking but not really *handsome.* That night, after talking about two or three hours together, we retired to George's room and took a long talk over tobacco pipes about former days and other scenes. The chimney to George's "office" or "studio," or "room" (as you please for it was all) took fire, and we had quite a time putting it out, but finally succeeded. We retired late expecting to leave for town early next morning.[5]

FRIDAY, JANUARY 16TH

Got up and dressed soon after daylight this morning, expecting to start immediately, but Miss Tillie, having breakfast about ready, insisted that we could not leave, so we stayed for breakfast and found the carriage in readiness to take us down to the river. We shook hands with both and promised to call again, if we should ever be in the vicinity of Jackson, and were soon off for town.

Reached the "Confederate House" by eight or half after and found that the train would not leave before twelve midnight and was very sorry that we had not remained in the country longer. Finally the train started with one car. We succeeded in getting a seat. Brown had got a bottle of Peach Brandy and fires being very poor and the car open we all took on a little thinking it would do no harm.

Reached Vicksburg about dark and went straight through to camp without further delay.

SATURDAY, JANUARY 17TH (VICKSBURG)

Spent the day in issuing and felt a little *blue* after so much good fun. Retired early tonight.

SUNDAY, JANUARY 18TH

Nothing of any great interest, the day being spent in reading my Bible and a sermon from Capt. Crouch.[6]

MONDAY, JANUARY 19TH

Issuing was the principal employment of the day.

TUESDAY, JANUARY 20TH

Reading and writing was the order of the day.

SATURDAY, FEBRUARY 14TH

Sent no valentines but got up a goodly number for some of the other boys.

WEDNESDAY, FEBRUARY 18TH

Received today from home by the kindness of Cousin Nick Earnest a pair of very nice janes pants, a letter from Pa, and a pair of wool gloves from Aunt Julia Stephens. Tate got some ham, turkey, biscuit, etc. from home and we had quite a good time eating it. Last, but by no means least, we got a cake in partnership (Tate and I) made and sent us by the fair hands of our little black eyed friend Miss H. Bell Maxwell. It was cheering, indeed, to know that my good old Aunt had not forgotten me and that there was still a green spot for us in the memory of the fair.[7]

THURSDAY, FEBRUARY 19TH

After three gloomy, wet days, we were again greeted this morning with a beautiful, most cheering sunshine. The Lt. Col. went to town and succeeded in getting a fresh ham and a little bucket full of lard for which he paid the *very moderate price* of *twenty dollars.* We were glad enough to get it at that price as we had eaten no meat for several days—the beef being literally *unfit for use.* Our only diet had been *corn bread.* We had plenty of molasses, but I didn't dare eat them on account of Diarrhea.

We returned our compliments to Miss Bell with an acknowledgment of the nice present received.

> *Well before the privation caused by the siege, the soldiers' food supply clearly was less than the best. On March 18, a soldier in Company F of the Sixtieth wrote home "we drawed beef a while back so poor when it was boiled it made good glue."*[8]

Friday, February 20th

Arose early this morning and found the prospect good for a pretty spring day. Spent the day in looking about—issuing etc. The Yanks from some unknown cause did not shell the city any today. No mail today—we have had none for several days.

Saturday, February 21st

Was a cloudy, damp day. I read some in Byron-issued rations and wrote a letter to Pa. We were not disturbed in any way by the Yanks today.

In the evening the clouds blew away and we had a beautiful, moonlight night. I strolled off to the top of one of the surrounding ridges to enjoy the scene, and gave way to reverie for a time. The scene was one calculated to charm an admirer of nature and excite a lively imagination. One of those strange dreamy kind of evenings which brings out the memory of other days and happier ones—transports one to happy times and steals the hours away unawares.

Sunday, February 22nd

Got up this morning and found it rather pleasant—a little cloudy, but rather too cool for rain. I had a little business to attend to in town, and concluded to attend the services at some church and accordingly put on the best clothes I could muster.

When I got over, as I passed up Washington Street I met Capt. R. Roddie and talked with him a little while. Passed on and was introduced to Col. Gillespie—he looks quite a clever portly gentleman.

As I passed the Catholic church, services were just opening, so I concluded to step in and see them through, as I had never visited one of their churches. The building is one of the nicest churches I ever visited, ornamented with images of the Virgin Mary and the Apostles. Everything was mystery. The light coming through red and blue glass, the seven huge candles burning, the Priest with his blue robe and huge, gilt embroidered cross, together with the little boys attending in white robes, the "chimes," all, all was *mysterious*.

The music was fine, the organ one of the best I ever saw. Most of the congregation were Irish and very rough. A few French were also present who were neat and well dressed.

Called to see Will McNabb as I came back, found him much better—about able to return to camp. Being late dinner time, I took dinner at the house where he was boarding.

About an hour "by sun," I took a stroll with Tate to the top of a neighboring hill. After looking around for some time we seated ourselves on a huge oak stump some four feet in diameter and talked of things "past, present & future." Meanwhile the sun had run down nearly to the horizon, presenting as lovely a scene as ever eye looked upon. From our position, running in a curve to the right was a range of sharp crested hills, shooting up almost perpendicularly to the height of two hundred feet, their sides beautifully shaded with over hanging cane and small trees. From the top of the giddy heights on our left could be seen the dark outlines of huge collumbiads and the sentinel walking his lonely rounds. The broad sheet of the Mississippi spread out in front while a winding brook poured through the little valley into the great expanse of water like a silvery cord dangling from a huge gilt sheet. Upon this panorama we watched the last rays of the sinking sun fall. Sitting here contemplating the scene half enchanted we were unmindful of the hour until roused by the drum for roll call.[9]

MONDAY, FEBRUARY 23RD

Nothing of great importance today—no mail yet! The Devil must certainly have got a position in the Postoffice Department.

Fixed up Lieut. Hunt's papers today for discharge.[10]

TUESDAY, FEBRUARY 24TH

Spent the morning in reading and writing. In the evening the mail came in—it was quite a large one, several hundred letters. Among others I received my share, in a lengthy one from Cousin "Puss." It has revived me considerably—was much gratified to find I was still remembered by my Brabsontown friends. Shall try and answer soon, at length. Nothing further of interest occurring during the day, I'll say no more concerning it.

WEDNESDAY, FEBRUARY 25TH

Arose this morning to find a rainy day setting in. This was what I expected as I had been up—called to the breastworks at midnight and returned about three this morning.

The day was principally taken up in reading an interesting romance, "The White Chief," by Capt. Mayne Reid.[11] Mail came in today, but none for me. Still raining at bedtime.

THURSDAY, FEBRUARY 26TH

When I got up this morning, I found that rain was still falling.

Finished "The White Chief"—it's the best novel I've seen in a long while.

In the evening some of the boys and I had a regular old ginger cake eating and beer drinking. After supper walked down to headquarters. Passed the evening in singing some songs, and finally winding up by a game of euchre.

Had a letter from Pa today.

FRIDAY, FEBRUARY 27TH

Spent a good portion of the day in making out pay rolls for Company K. No mail for the regiment today—not a letter. In the evening walked out to see some of the sick ones. Started a letter to "Puss," but as usual was interrupted in the beginning and had to abandon the idea for the present.

A deserter coming over today reports the enemy dying rapidly.

The day was wound up by an interesting game of "Whist." Nick Fain and Jake Miller were against Capt. Gammon and myself. They beat us the rub game, but we promised they should be treated in a similar manner the next opportunity.[12]

SATURDAY, FEBRUARY 28TH

Today was quite pleasant in the earlier part, but gave us a slight warning of the approach of March. Felt so dull and stupid that I did little of anything. Finished my letter to "Puss," but too late to mail it. No mail today. Went to bed early.

SUNDAY, MARCH 1ST

A beautiful day—bright and cheering. I spent the morning and forenoon lying about the encampment talking over the prospect of us all having smallpox, as a case had made its appearance this morning in Company E adjoining us.

Capt. Morrow and I went up to Mrs. Riddle's for dinner. By some mysterious chance everyone had got through and left before we got there and we had quite a nice time by ourselves. The old lady after awhile invited us in to dinner which was really nice. We had baked chicken, turkey, *good biscuit,* butter, tea & milk with a spotless white tablecloth to eat it on. Furthermore there was a witty little Scotchman to keep up the fun. I enjoyed it prodigiously. The good lady refused to accept any pay for it and said to "consider that we had *dined* with her today." I said "thank you I *shall.*"

Forgot to mail my letter until it was too late for the mail.

MONDAY, MARCH 2ND

Had another beautiful day. A real spring day. Read a little, fixed up descriptive rolls for some men going to the hospital and then, as a court-martial was to meet in our marquee, I gave way and went over and had a game of euchre with Nick Fain.

Commenced reading "A Long Look Ahead," or "The First Stroke and the Last One," by A. S. Roe.[13] After supper Will Rankin and I took a moonlight stroll.

Retired early and was awakened about 9 o'clock by Lieut. Ray who told us his brother was dead and he wished me to get up his papers for him to get off home with his remains. I of course consented and went out to where his brother was on the hill. Returned about twelve o'clock.[14]

Have a troublesome sore throat.

TUESDAY, MARCH 3RD

Another pretty day. Wrote a note to Pa by Lieut. Ray who is preparing to leave tomorrow with his brother's remains. Nothing further of importance.[15]

WEDNESDAY, MARCH 4TH

Today I did but little of anything, being unwell—decidedly bilious and very low spirited—with an entire aversion to everything eatable except such things as are acid.

THURSDAY, MARCH 5TH

Nothing of interest today. No mail.

FRIDAY, MARCH 6TH

Arose this morning tolerably early and looked around a little— still feel very badly—eat some tea and bread for breakfast, but before I had finished my stomach rebelled and it all came back again.

Today there was a division review. We were called upon to witness the saddest scene a soldier ever sees—to see a deserter meet his doom. Thomas Graham of the First Louisiana Artillery was the man we allude to. At the fall of Fort Jackson he was taken prisoner by the Federals and pardoned on honor—while on his parole he enlisted in the Seventh Maine Regiment. Was recaptured by us some time since and sentenced to be shot. There were also two others captured at the same time, one of which was executed before General Stephenson's Division, the other in presence of General Maury's Division. I did not learn their names.

Graham died like a soldier, without a murmur. He would not be tied or blindfolded. Escorted by the guard he walked out as if nothing were going on. When about twenty yards from the guard detailed for the execution, he was left by the guard, who filed to one side. He then lifted up his cap very gracefully and made a little speech to those immediately around him. Then replacing his cap he drew himself up to his full height and announced that he was ready. The commands were then given by the officer in charge—"Ready" "Aim" "Fire!" and the poor fellow without a struggle dropped to the earth a lifeless corpse.

As soon as the execution was over I returned to camp, being very weak and tired. On arriving, I found two letters for me, one from Tom Brabson at Shelbyville, Tenn. The other from my Rheatown friends. At bedtime it was quite cloudy.

Twin forts, Jackson and Saint Philips, intended to bar the approach to New Orleans, were situated on opposite sides of the Mississippi River, seventy miles down the river from the city. After a fierce naval battle, the forts were surrendered on April 28, 1862.

Thomas Graham had enlisted on February 28, 1861, as a private in Company B, First Louisiana Heavy Artillery.[16]

SATURDAY, MARCH 7TH

Arose this morning and found it had rained and almost washed everything away in our tent. I still feel very badly—fear my sickness may last several days.

After due consideration and consultation I determined to go to the country a few days and enjoy the cool air, graze a little, etc. for my health. By twelve A.M. all arrangements were completed and I started for Mr. Samuel Wall's, who had been recommended to me as a proper place to stay. After a weary tramp through the hot sun I reached the house, which is some four miles from camp. It is the most pleasantly situated locality I have seen for a dwelling around Vicksburg.

I found several of our boys boarding with Mr. W. By a little gentle persuasion, I got in and went into a room with Capt. Neale and Lieut. Martin. Bedding was scarce and I had brought none with me but after a little consultation Capt. & Lieut. very kindly offered me some of theirs, and I soon had all necessary arrangements made and "all right."[17]

At the supper table I was introduced to Mrs. W. and Miss Martha Wall (Mrs. M . . .), a grass widow, quite young and seemingly quite accomplished. I was pleased with the tidy appearance of everything about the table and the general air of neatness shown in everything around. As I am quite weak and tired I will retire early.[18]

An interlined note in the first paragraph of this entry, in a different ink, was apparently added later: "turned out to be a case of catarrhal jaundice," now known as viral hepatitis.[19]

SUNDAY, MARCH 8TH

Arose this morning, after a terrible night's tussle with the "corkscrews" in my bed, feeling rather the "worse 'o the wear." Sat around for several hours feeling too badly to either read or write. Tate Earnest and Adjt. Newman came out to see me about eleven o'clock and remained until after dinner.[20]

In the evening Capt. Blair came out and stayed with us. He and I put an old dry hide on our case of springs and found it a great improvement, slept tolerably well. Felt very badly when I retired.[21]

MONDAY, MARCH 9TH

Still unwell—felt no better this morning. Spent the day in sitting about the room, reading a little occasionally. Feel so weak and spiritless that I have no disposition to do anything. Took some blue mass and retired early.

Blue mass, a favored treatment for intestinal disorders, was a compound of mercury and ground chalk.[22]

TUESDAY, MARCH 10TH

When I arose this morning I felt but little better—jaundice is still visible very plainly in my eyes and face.

During last night it rained almost incessantly—about twelve or one o'clock at night, we heard heavy firing in the direction of town—supposed to be a boat passing.

The day was quite gloomy and we were all confined to the house. I felt very badly all day and therefore did but little of anything.

WEDNESDAY, MARCH 11TH

During the forenoon I felt better, but spoiled it all at dinner by eating too much.

Will Rankin and Tate came out to see me today and stayed several hours. After they left I undertook to read Shakespeare's "Tempest," but soon laid it down feeling quite exhausted.

We have quite a time with "Uncle Wesley" and the other "colored friends" getting anything done. Wesley is a fair specimen of a southern Negro; always going to do something for you as soon as he does something else. Tell him to bring up some wood and he is certain to reply, "yes sir, yes sir soon as I take some water in to Mrs. Sam," and that is the last you see of him for some time.[23]

Thursday, March 12th

Arose this morning just in time for breakfast feeling considerably better than I did yesterday. Spent the early portion of the day in reading and writing a letter to Pa.

In the afternoon, Captain Neale, Lt. Martin and I went a hunting. I killed a squirrel and then we got a rabbit up and had quite a nice chase. I got a shot at him but was so nervous that I missed him. However Dan and the rest of the pack did better for they strung him up. We then returned to speculate on the prospect of Rabbit soup.

Being somewhat wearied with the chase I retired early.

Friday, March 13th

Spent the day up to dinner in walking around and reading a little. Finished "The Tempest"—it is a very interesting play, and shows a thorough knowledge of the customs of every branch of society known at that time.

Allen Wash came out from camp and brought me two letters, one from Pa, the other from sister containing two steel worked badges.

In the afternoon, Allen and I struck out for a rabbit hunt—we caught one and had another very pretty chase.

We all had a very long social talk and some anecdotes from Capt. Neale after supper.

Saturday, March 14th

In the morning after making a note or two I walked around a little—cut my initials on a tree in the lot etc., and returned to the house. Wrote to Cousin Kate at Rheatown.

Captains Blair and Neale having returned from an excursion to the Battlefield, and Lieutenant Gammon and Tate having come out from camp we had quite a lively time during the afternoon with talking, playing euchre, and some good music on the violin by Lieut. G.

After supper we all adjourned to the parlour where we were met by Mr. Wall and several others—had some more music. I was struck with the effect produced on a pet dog of Miss Mattie's—he seemed perfectly delighted with it and could scarcely be gotten out and after he was out he still lingered around the door wagging his tail.

SUNDAY, MARCH 15TH

Sat around this morning for some time reading my Bible— begin to think of going to camp. After dinner Will Rankin and Capt. McClure called to see me.

As Capt. Neale was going to camp I concluded to go with him (as I had certain reasons for doing so). Started out afoot, and when within a mile and a half of camp it commenced raining and give us a good wetting.

MONDAY, MARCH 16TH

This morning I was up early and out talking to the boys, an election having been ordered in Company K for Brevette 2nd lieutenant. My opponent, S. W. McInterff, was busy as a bee, but all to no avail, for at nine o'clock when the vote was read out I was Lieutenant, Company K, 79th Regiment, Tennessee Volunteers.

This transaction relieved me of a long suspense, as I had long expected it and was anxious to have it off of my mind. Not that I was so very anxious for the position, but having determined to run I wished it to be settled and over with.

TUESDAY, MARCH 17TH

The day was occupied in moving our encampment further up into the woods. We got quite a nice cabin for our marquee and good bunks to sleep on. We improved our circumstances considerably by the move. Was very tired by the time roll call came on so I retired early.

WEDNESDAY, MARCH 18TH

Wrote to Pa this morning spent the day in looking around as I have not reported for duty yet.

THURSDAY, MARCH 19TH

Reported for duty this morning. Was put in charge of a detail of fifteen men and ordered to report to Maj. Gillespie of Vicksburg for fatigue duty.

After knocking around the depot, loading sugar etc., until after twelve, I started down town and called at a restaurant and made my dinner off of oyster soup and crackers. In the afternoon I had nothing to do so I layed around until four o'clock and marched my men back to camp. Felt tired enough to sleep when I arrived so by eight o'clock I retired. Met Lockhart, an old Emory acquaintance.

FRIDAY, MARCH 20TH

Slept like a log last night, got up early this morning and attended roll call, felt very much refreshed by my nights sleep. Spent about two hours of the forenoon drilling battalion drill.

After dinner I borrowed Lt. Col. Gregg's horse and rode out to Genl. Wall's after my satchel, which had been left when I came in. I got some cuttings of the yellow jassamine and one or two rose slips to send home by Lt. Conley. By the time night came I was ready for bed so I tumbled in but was aroused once or twice by an alarm but retired again as we could find out nothing about it.[24]

SATURDAY, MARCH 21ST

Lieutenant Conley started home this morning. I sent the cuttings and wrote a note to Uncle Ben by him. Received a letter from sister Maria. Wrote to sister Beck. Had a fine day—quite warm, fortunately it was wash day and we had no drill.[25]

In the evening I had a game at quoits. Retired at eight and slept quite soundly.

Sunday, March 22nd

Spent the fore noon in reading my Bible and writing a letter to Tom Brabson. Also read a little more in "A Long Look Ahead," so long abandoned.

In the afternoon George McNabb and I walked over to Rowan's regiment to see the boys. John O Cannon has returned and was on hand. We had a long talk about the friends in Tennessee and things in general.[26]

I retired early after singing a while in Capt. Gammon's marquee, this being my night to go to the trenches and a very gloomy prospect ahead.

Received a very beautiful bouquet from a lady in the country today.

Monday, March 23rd

At twelve last night I was aroused by the drum and had to get out of bed and start to the trenches a mile distant in the midst of a very heavy rain. We had no very pleasant time of it, as the night was as dark as a pile of ravens, and the road as bad as one usually finds, being over hills almost perpendicular, perfectly sleek with mud and beset on every side with little stumps and brush, to say nothing at all about wading the creeks and mud shoe mouth deep in the ravines.

After remaining in the trenches until daylight, without sleeping a wink, we returned to camps with a hearty relish for our breakfast. When breakfast was over we read an hour or two, becoming tired and the rain forbidding all outdoor exercise Lieut. Fain and I had a very pleasant game of euchre by which time the rain had ceased.

About this time an incessant roll of very heavy artillery commenced in the direction of town, occasioned perhaps by the sloop "Hartford" coming in sight of our batteries.[27]

Received a letter from Pa saying that he had started me a barrel of flour and a box of provisions—glorious news this.

TUESDAY, MARCH 24TH

Arose this morning just in time for breakfast. After breakfast I stirred around awhile and spent most of the time between that and noon in reading. Spent the afternoon in reading, pitching horse shoes etc.

WEDNESDAY, MARCH 25TH

Last night being quite cool, I awoke this morning just before dawn quite cold—was just thinking of getting an additional blanket from Capt. Morrow's bed, as he was gone to the works, when I heard a signal gun fire and then commenced a continual roar of artillery; our drum beat the alarm, signals having been given from Gen. Vaughn's quarters.

We hastened into our position at the pits. It was daylight by the time we got there. We saw two gun boats passing. They had got by the position we occupied before our arrival. The batteries were playing on them from all sides and they were already crippled so as not to be able to run but were just floating along at ease.

After watching anxiously for half an hour we saw that one of them was sinking, a little longer and we saw the men jumping overboard. They were evidently abandoning her—a shout rent the air which was repeated again and again by our boys, and finally she settled down to the bottom of the Mississippi.

The other boat is evidently disabled—she can not be worked at all or she would have gone to the assistance of the one that just sank. She has been penetrated by several shots from our guns and drifts up to the Louisiana shore in all probability so far a wreck as to be of no use to the enemy in its present situation.

We left them in this condition and returned with the regiment to camp, having a considerable inclination to eat breakfast. A good morning's work this.[28]

Spent the time until dinner reading "A Long Look Ahead"; after dinner I finished it. I was much pleased with the work. At the beginning it has nothing exciting but a kind of cheerful pleasantry is visible which bespeaks ones interest to know more of it. As a whole it is very well planned, the later scenes being of the most exciting character, and exhibits a good deal of skill and complete command of language on the part of the author.

Had a game of quoits in the evening, at sundown attended dress parade.

Retired pretty early. Sam Crawford returned. Brought me a letter from Pa.

THURSDAY, MARCH 26TH

Spent most of the fore-noon in drilling some new recruits in the manual of arms, no very pleasant job. After dinner I wrote to Uncle Will Cannon. Had no battalion drill this evening, as tomorrow is the day set apart by the president for fasting and prayer, and the Colonel gave the boys this evening to prepare for it.

FRIDAY, MARCH 27TH

Today, after returning from the works where I had gone in charge of a squad at twelve last night—I ate breakfast and prepared for going to head quarters and attend divine services. Rev. W. H. Crawford led in the services. We also had some remarks from Col. Pitts and Rev. Mr. Renfrow.[29]

It was near two o'clock before we returned to camp, and as we sent our cook around after some milk Capt. and I had to get dinner—he made the bread and I cooked the meat. It was a perfect success and as good as the cook or anyone else could have done.

After dinner Captain Morrow and I had quite a snug little game of euchre. Went over and had a long talk with Lieutenant Spears (just returned from an expedition up the Yazoo) about his trip. I regret that circumstances were such that I could not go with him.[30]

Saturday, March 28th

Had an alarm this morning about half past three o'clock and a good tramp to the breastworks. The alarm proved to be false. Just at daylight we heard heavy firing in the direction of Warrenton— sounded like it might be a few broadsides from the schooner Hartford. I went in company with the rest of our officers to General Vaughn's headquarters to consider subjects in which the brigade is interested.

From head quarters Lieut. Allen, Lieut. Lotsfitch and I went to town. I found my barrel of flour had arrived from Tenn. We called and took some eggs and oyster soup at a restaurant. Looked around a little while and returned to camp.[31]

After supper we had quite a nice game of euchre in Capt. Gammon's marquee. Retired soon after roll call.

Warrenton was on the river, south of Vicksburg.

Sunday, March 29th

About twelve o'clock last night we were aroused by cries and a tremendous noise outside. At first we thought it was an alarm, but soon found that we had mistaken the crash of falling timber for the roar of cannon. As hastily as possible we arose and dressed.

When we opened the door a dreadful scene met us. The night was black as adamant, the wind swept by in a perfect hurricane, and a roar like continual, distant thunder. Intermingled with the uproar of the elements was the crash of falling timber, the groans of the wounded and the frantic screams of terrified men running back and forth in perfect confusion. There was something in the scene terribly sublime, it was a visible, feeling vindication of His Majesty Who directs the Storm.

We were all busily engaged until nearly morning hunting up and getting out the wounded and seeing after our friends. The whole loss when we got everything straitened and examined we found to be were six killed and three badly crippled, beside others slightly hurt. After daylight commenced the process of cutting down the timber which continued all day.

At night I retired early being quite sleepy. Orderly Sergeant Bowman of Company F died today of smallpox—a heavy draw on our regiment this, seven in a day.[32]

Earnest's casualty count may refer only to his regiment. In any case, the storm killed at least six men in a brigade that had only eight or nine men killed during the siege, May 18–July 4, 1863.

Monday, March 30th

The day was spent principally in cutting timber and clearing up the encampment, arranging matters for the men to sleep etc. We had Capts. Bacon and Hodges, Major Rhea and Dr. Earnest with us for dinner today. Quite a dreary day—windy and quite cool. Retired before nine.[33]

Tuesday, March 31st

At one o'clock this morning I went to the works with my squad. Spent most of the time between eight and twelve o'clock in writing a letter to Pa and making out some descriptive lists. After noon I read some and looked around a little.

WEDNESDAY, APRIL 1ST

Slept splendidly last night. This being the first day of the month, Col. Gregg "played off" on me, but, we paid him off in his own coin before the day was out. Drilled company drill in the forenoon and battalion drill after-noon. Went to bed before nine.

THURSDAY, APRIL 2ND

Got up this morning to roll call. At nine o'clock we started out on Division inspection (or rather, review). We were reviewed by Gen. M. L. Smith. The 2nd Brigade did splendidly, especially our regiment.

Gen Smith is quite a fine looking man—perfectly straight—a placid countenance, but expressive of great firmness. He looks to be about forty-five years old—his hair just beginning to silver—his height is medium and rather heavy set.

It was about two o'clock when we returned. After dinner we fixed up several old accounts made by the commissary department at Waynesville and forwarded them to Capt. W. A. Crawford. We earnestly hope this will be the last of these old accounts.

Spent the beautiful moonlight evening before my cabin listening to some good music off on the right wing.

Received two letters from Pa today.

In addition to commanding the division of which Vaughn's brigade was a part, Martin Luther Smith, trained as an engineer at West Point, was one of those responsible for the construction of Vicksburg's defenses.

FRIDAY, APRIL 3RD

Got up this morning at roll call. Drilled company drill this morning and battalion drill after noon. Col. like to have forgotten to stop this evening on battalion drill. Some of the boys growled a good deal, but I thought it altogether in place.

Read some today in the life of Charles I. Nothing further of particular interest transpiring, I retired soon after tatoo.

SATURDAY, APRIL 4TH

The morning was spent in looking around, not doing much of anything. Lieut. Mel Smith called and remained with us until after dinner.

We then started out in search of an adventure. Called at a house and called for some water. The old gentleman invited us in, gave us some water and as there was a piano and guitar, with a couple of young ladies to match, at hand, we took seats. After talking for some time, we ventured to ask one of them to play for us. She readily complied—gave us some thrilling airs and a little of the instrumental. Before leaving we found that the Misses Bowie were the ladies we had met up with. They gave us a very cordial invitation to call again.

SUNDAY, APRIL 5TH

Arose at roll call. After breakfast I went down to Capt. Hodges' marquee and Lieutenants Britt and McBride concluded to go to preaching with me in town. We attended the Catholic services —had a very good sermon and a good prayer. Just before the services closed a flag of truce came down from the Federal fleet. We can not divine the cause of it.[34]

Came back to camp pretty late and took on a heavy dinner. Rev. Mr. Atkins preached for us this evening—being very tired I did not go out. Retired early.

MONDAY, APRIL 6TH

Drilling was the order of the day. Before noon Adjutant and I took the company through company drill. Lieut. Hunt was down today and stayed all night. No mail for me today. The weather fine, rather too warm for drilling.

TUESDAY, APRIL 7TH

A beautiful day and well put in at drilling. No mail for me today.

After supper we had a meeting of the commissioned officers of the regiment for the purpose of organizing a debating society. Capt. Gammon was called to the chair and appointed me to assist as secretary, etc. Retired as soon as the meeting adjourned, this being my night to visit the breastworks.

> *Brief minutes of the meetings of April 7 and April 13 survive. The first meeting was organizational, with election of officers and appointment of committees; the most notable action was a motion of thanks to Colonel Gregg for offering his room as a meeting place.*

WEDNESDAY, APRIL 8TH

Drilled heavily today. Received two letters from Tennessee today, one from "Puss" and one from Rheatown. It was quite refreshing to hear from my friends again—as these are the first letters I have received in a long while. Nothing further of importance occurring I retired early as we were expecting an alarm.

THURSDAY, APRIL 9TH

Wrote to Pa and sent the letter by Lieutenant Stonecypher who has been discharged on account of white swelling.[35]

FRIDAY, APRIL 10TH

We drilled before and after dinner. Late in the evening a wagon arrived from town bringing out my boxes of provision. On opening them I found everything snugly stored and in good order—they were well filled with such things as would be very refreshing to a hungry man.

SATURDAY, APRIL 11TH

No drill today. In the morning took John Holmes down to be examined by the senior surgeon (Dr. Pitts). Did not get back until after dinner. Paid off the company this morning up to the 28th of February. Received a letter from Tom Brabson.

SUNDAY, APRIL 12TH

After awaiting all night at the trenches, in the midst of a heavy rain, for the approach of the enemy, we were at length relieved by the approach of daylight and returned to camp. The day was a gloomy one. Parson Alexander preached for us in the evening but having lost so much sleep the night before I did not go out to hear him. Wrote two letters this morning, one to Pa and one to cousin Eliza B.

MONDAY, APRIL 13TH

Drilling was the order of the day. Nothing of interest occurred.

The second of the two recorded meetings of the debating society was held on this day. For reasons not stated, a new slate of officers was elected, but with Earnest continuing as secretary. The Committee on Constitution reported, and the constitution was adopted. The Committee on Questions reported. The question for the next meeting was "Has the Blockade of our Forts been productive of good or evil to the Confederacy?" Two members each were appointed for the affirmative and negative sides.

TUESDAY, APRIL 14TH

Went down to see Dr. Pitts this morning on some business from there to town. Saw Miss Emma in town and bowed to her, but had no opportunity of conversing with her. On my return to camp found two letters for me, one from Pa and one from Sister. Nothing further of interest.

WEDNESDAY, APRIL 15TH

Drilled today and wrote a letter to sister. This being our night to go to the breastworks I retired early.

THURSDAY, APRIL 16TH

Drilled today and went through the ordinary routine of camp duty. Was awakened last night by the boys shouting outside. Got up and found we were ordered to cook five days rations and be ready for leaving by nine o'clock this morning. I slept no more but went to work getting ready. By the time specified all were ready but we were kept waiting for several hours, when an order came for us to hold ourselves in readiness to move at any moment. The day wore on in this manner. Retired early as we had lost a good deal of sleep the night before.[36]

3

Campaign and Siege

It seems that we are to do our sleeping in day time. This morning about three o'clock we were roused by an alarm. By the time we got fairly started the river batteries were in full blast and a continual roar of artillery from our lines cheered us as we advanced in quick time to our positions. In our road we were greeted by a few shells from the gun boats but they passed harmlessly over our heads, one exploding in about fifty yards of our company.

We found that the enemy were passing some gunboats and we had the pleasure of seeing one of them in flames from stem to stern, and another one was sunk.

Came to camp about daylight. Had Battalion drill this evening. Nothing further of importance occurred. Retired early.

Was in a court-martial this evening as judge advocate.

General Grant's determination to confront Pemberton at Vicksburg led him in several directions. His December campaign, including Sherman's direct assault on the northern approaches, had failed.

Now he planned to march down the western bank of the Mississippi, transport his troops across the river below Vicksburg, and come back up to the fortress from the south and east. This was a daring plan, because, once across the river, Grant would have great difficulty in maintaining any regular supply line and would have to take with him substantially all military supplies that he needed, at least for the early stages of the campaign.

But the first challenge was moving his transports down past Vicksburg in order to ferry men across the river. First, there were efforts on the western bank of the Mississippi to find a way for ships through the bayous and back to the river below Vicksburg. Even with the added exhausting attempt at digging a canal, no way could be found. Finally, Grant and Adm. David Porter agreed to run the transports down the river past Vicksburg's formidable artillery.

On the night of April 16, Porter led the first attempt. Eleven gunboats and transports, darkened, decks padded with sacks of grain and bales of hay and cotton, and muffled as much as possible, started out in a single line. The night was clear and dark at the 10:30 departure, and the high banks shading the river made its surface even darker.

Confederate pickets in small boats sounded the alarm, and the batteries on the bluff came to life. Buildings on the western shore were fired, giving a backlight to aid the gunners' aim. One observer counted 525 shells fired from Vicksburg during the ninety-minute passage, or one about every ten seconds.[1]

By midnight, the passage was complete. All of the ships were damaged, and one was destroyed, but there was no loss of life and only thirteen men were wounded. During the night of April 22, six more transports were run down, and one was lost. Again, the Federals suffered no fatalities and only a few wounded. Grant now had the transports that he needed.

Admiral Porter had warned Grant that, once the boats had been brought down, there would be no way to get them back up against the current and under fire. This did not concern Grant, who was looking forward and not over his shoulder.

It is curious that Earnest refers to a three o'clock alarm, since by then the ships were well past the city and the guns were silent.

SATURDAY, APRIL 18TH

Arose this morning at roll call, dressed and sat around until breakfast. After breakfast we sat about reading a little and writing some. After noon I copied the constitution of "The Regimental [*unintelligible*]" and recorded the minutes of last meeting.

About sundown Brian Stephens arrived. We walked after supper and talked over the occurrences of the day etc. We then got up a game of euchre and had quite a nice time. About ten o'clock it commenced raining and rousted some of the boys out of their holes. Lt. Col. Gregg, Jim Crawford, and Cornelius Luckey came over and took shelter with us so we had quite a house full.

The dim text for this entry makes one word unintelligible, possibly a reference to the debating society. However, there may have been other groups meeting formally.

SUNDAY, APRIL 19TH

Arose this morning about roll call and by the time I was ready—the breakfast was on the table. The General had us out at the breastworks at nine o'clock this morning for Gen. Smith to see us and see how long it would take us to get there in case of an alarm.

When I returned I found Brian still on hand—we sat about talking until after dinner, when he had to start to his regiment. I walked down as far as Col. Pitts' regiment with him. Retired tolerably early tonight feeling a little fatigued by my walk.

MONDAY, APRIL 20TH

Nothing of particular interest occurred. Drilled as usual. No mail today for me.

TUESDAY, APRIL 21ST

Arose this morning at reveille and ate breakfast. Prepared to go out on inspection before Major Geralt. (Gen. Smith's inspector general)

Made an awful out at the start, Col. C. making a complete mess of it. Col. Gregg then took charge of the battalion and soon got things straightened. Major G. then took us through awhile, the boys performing very well. After a drill of about four hours we returned to camp.[2]

Soon after we had eaten dinner rain commenced falling and continued until about sundown. This being our night to man the works, we started out just before dark and a time we had which we hope will not soon be repeated. The mud was shoe mouth deep and perfectly sticky. The hillsides were slick as glass and the air sultry, oppressively warm. I got a very convenient place to sleep in Gen. Vaughn's passage.

Wednesday, April 22nd

Returned to camp this morning as soon as day had fairly dawned and brought with me a beautiful bouquet composed principally of various verbenas which I culled in the yard of Gen. Vaughn's headquarters.

Tate went to the country today, being threatened with an attack of bilious fever. Drilled battalion drill in the afternoon. Retired early.

Had a charm doctor to work on my warts. He made quite an exhibition of his mystic art. Will see how it comes out.

Thursday, April 23rd

Had an alarm last night about eleven o'clock and we all double-quicked it to the works. When we got there the whole line of batteries, along the river, were ablaze and the boom of artillery rang through the air like incessant thunder. Soon after our arrival our men fired a house on the opposite side of the river which lit up the whole scene. Six boats passed in succession. They were doubtless struck by several shots from our batteries, but as to the extent of the damage I am unable to say. Nothing further of interest.

This was the second and final phase of Admiral Porter's move downriver.

Friday, April 24th

Made out a muster roll this morning; my arm being very much inflamed from vaccination I quit the business.

Will Rankin and I, after dinner was over, rode out to see Tate, at Capt. Edwards.

Had a slight idea of calling on the road back—but concluded to defer it until another time. Found Tate in the best of quarters, and improving rapidly. Carried him a letter from Cousin Vic. No news of particular importance. Was introduced to Dr. Cook while at the Captains'.

Returned to camp about dark. Retired early.

Saturday, April 25th

My arm still no better today. Did not drill, this being wash day with the men. Owing to a Yankee raid on the Southern R.R. we received no mail today—they (the Yanks) captured—it is said—a mail train and I think a letter or two in the lot they got was for "myself"—but no harm they will not be likely to enjoy the contents if they get them.

Nothing of particular interest occurring I shall slide to another day. Went to the ditches this evening.

As it was early when I got out there I walked over to the brigade commissary and talked to the boys awhile. Received an invitation from Ferd Naff to sleep in his house whenever it should suit my convenience. It will be apt to *suit* rainy nights.

Sunday, April 26th

Returned to camp early this morning. After breakfast Will Rankin and I rode out to see Tate again. On our arrival we found him about as usual—improving rapidly. We were introduced to

Lt. Edwards (of —— artillery) soon after our arrival. We spent the time very pleasantly until dinner.

At the dinner table we were introduced to Capt. Edwards & lady also to Mrs. Lt. Edwards and Miss Mattie Edwards. We had two *delicacies* at the table (beside the substantials and good company) viz. *green peas* and *strawberries and cream*. I was very much taken with Miss Mattie, as well as the dinner. I saw more real hospitality at Capt. E's than I have experienced since I came to Vicksburg.

About four o'clock we set out for camp with the intention of calling at Dr. C's, but seeing the young ladies by the road side and I having Tate's satchel, we concluded to abandon the project until another time. I had a peep at the young ladies. Think from the glance I had I would admire Miss Portia. As the others were in the back ground, I had but small opportunity of seeing them.

Monday, April 27th

Received notice yesterday evening to report with my sword at headquarters by seven this morning—did so and found that I was to take charge of a guard going to town. I reported to Capt. Woodward at the *Roundhouse*.

After posting my guard, I betook myself to thinking how to employ the spare moments. Seeing a young lady out on a neighboring piazza I concluded to *borrow a book* from her. (as that would be the most plausible excuse to get there and introduce myself) No sooner conjured up than done. I found her to be quite accomplished and had quite a long tete a tete with her.

She loaned me "The Homestead on the Hillside" by Mrs. M. J. Holmes.[3] The plan of this work is very ingenious and told in a very suitable way. "Senoro" is quite a novel character—but one that occasionally occurs in nature.

Spent the day in reading and looking after my guard. By the kindness of a gentleman belonging to the 3rd Tennessee I was furnished a very comfortable hammock and slept like a log.

TUESDAY, APRIL 28TH

Called on my lady friend this morning about eight and returned her book, passed a few pleasant words with her and bade her adieu with my kindest wishes. She invited me to call again.

Was relieved about nine o'clock and started for camp. Met Lt. Col. Gregg, Capt. Rankin, and G. R. McNabb in town. I stopped at the gunsmith's to have my pistol repaired. As I had to wait an hour the time was spent in looking around town with Col., Will and George.

When I got to camp I found the muster rolls were to be made out, so I let myself in and did the thing up in short order. By the time night came I was ready for bed.

WEDNESDAY, APRIL 29TH

The Regiment was inspected this morning in a most desperately hot sun. We bore it like heroes and stood our ground.

Today a fight was progressing below town near Grand Gulf on our extreme left. Latest accounts say the enemy were repulsed.

I received a letter today from Pa—all were well. Nothing of further interest today.

> *Grand Gulf lay downriver from Vicksburg. Grant and his army were assembled across the river at Hard Times. If Admiral Porter had been able to outgun the Confederates at Grand Gulf, Grant planned to cross there. However, the Federal gunboats in a five-hour duel only proved that Grand Gulf was as impregnable from the river as Vicksburg. Grant marched his army a few miles farther downriver and crossed at Bruinsburg.*[4]

THURSDAY, APRIL 30TH

This morning as soon as daylight dawned we came in from the trenches. After breakfast I went over to the medical department. As my arm is very slow getting well where I was vaccinated, I pulled off the scab and cauterized it. Had no drill this evening. After noon I walked over to General Vaughn's head quarters.

The Yankees are shelling away at Snider's Bluff. They will not be apt to fool anyone as that is undoubtedly a feint. Tomorrow morning we think the ball will open in good earnest—if not tomorrow perhaps the next day. We cannot in all probability escape a fight many days longer.

All right let them come—the quicker commenced the quicker it will be over.

> *The amateur strategist from East Tennessee may have recognized the attack as a feint, but his superiors did not. Gen. Carter Stevenson surveyed the action and sent word to Pemberton that the threat at Haynes Bluff and Snyder's Bluff was real. Pemberton then ordered men already on their way to Grand Gulf to countermarch back to Vicksburg. Grant made his crossing at Bruinsburg in the face of only token opposition.[5]*

Friday, May 1st

May dawns upon us with a smile. She comes like a sunbeam after a storm. Welcome May, with your sunshine, your green trees and your flowers. The day passed off perfectly quiet, more like Sunday than anything I've seen in some time.

In the morning I walked down to the brigade commissary, but found nothing there to be bought which I wanted. Went by Col. Pitts' regiment and attended to some business for the Company. Called at Capt. Lynche's battery to make some inquiries about JL Moire.

After my return I had my sore arm cauterized again. In the evening Dr. Mead gave some little warts on my hand a thorough burning which was quite painful for a while.

We have information that our forces repulsed the Yankees below Grand Gulf.

No mail today. A beautiful night.

SATURDAY, MAY 2ND

Nothing of particular interest from below today. Reports and rumors are afloat, but nothing official. We had nothing of interest today. We took our positions at the

This last, incomplete sentence is lined through.
Grant's crossing at Bruinsburg on April 30 was not yet general knowledge. Gen. Pemberton had been informed on April 30 of Grant's crossing and on May 1 of the loss of Port Gibson.[6]

SUNDAY, MAY 3RD

We spent the day in lying around camp. In the evening the heat was almost insufferable. I took "Nelson on Infidelity" and attempted to read some under a large shade tree—finally had to give it up on account of the mosquitoes.[7] We marched out to our position in the trenches and coiled up for a sleep on our blankets. Received a letter from Pa.

MONDAY, MAY 4TH

Were awakened last night about one o'clock by the firing of the pickets and soon found that a boat was coming down from the Yankee fleet. She ran so near to the shore on this side that we thought for a time that we might have something to do as she would try to land. But we were soon satisfied on that point by seeing her change direction "by the right oblique," and steam off across the river.

In the mean time our batteries had not been silent but were pouring the shot into her rapidly. Just as she was passing the lower batteries and hope of her being destroyed had almost vanished we had the pleasure of seeing the flames break out on her and in a few moments she was on fire from stem to stern.

Soon after she passed we received orders to cook four days rations and be in readiness to leave at a moment's warning. The day was spent in camp.

TUESDAY, MAY 5TH

Went out to Chickasaw Bayou on picket this evening. As soon as we got the men posted, I took a fish—had some glorious nibbles and could see alligator gars jumping up all around me but only succeeded in catching a small perch. Some of the gars jumping around in the water were five or six feet long and would probably weigh 20 pounds.

After fishing an hour or two I began to want my supper so I started for the lower post where my haversack was. On the road I struck a flourishing patch of dewberries, and had quite a treat, these being the first I had seen this year.

It was dark by the time I found the Captain. As soon as we had eaten a snack and visited the lower posts, we threw down our blankets and crawled in. I had hardly settled myself when the mosquitos commenced a furious attack on me. I fought them long and well, but it was all "no go" and was at length compelled to fall back behind my blanket.

I at first left a small hole next to the ground to breath through, but the winged forces soon flanked me and then my only alternative was to cover up head and ears. This movement completely fooled them for a time, but they pulled the cover off of me as soon as I was asleep, and when I awoke, I was squalling "murder! murder!"

A huge old mosquito with claws like a ground hog and a bill half as long as a sergeant's sword was seated on my shoulder trying to run his bill through my neck and pin me to the ground—fortunately it had lodged against my backbone and before he could make another trial the sentinel came to my relief at a "charge bayonets"—when "old sketer" flew off saying he "would be happy to repeat the call."

I sincerely hoped he would not. I now set about tucking the cover under me all around and finally went to sleep again. About daylight I was awakened by a tremendous roar—when I found the mosquitoes had pulled me to the edge of the bayou, and an old alligator jubilant at the prospect of getting me for his breakfast had given a tremendous laugh which awoke me, and I preferring not to be his breakfast shifted from there. I vowed never to allow myself to sleep on that bayou's bank again.

Mosquitoes, and indeed the climate along the Mississippi, were a hardship, especially for mountain boys. For a parallel account of trial by mosquito, see the diary of Calvin Smith, of the Thirty-first Tennessee.[8]

WEDNESDAY, MAY 6TH

Spent most of the day in fishing and hunting berries. We were relieved about one o'clock in the evening and returned to camp.

THURSDAY, MAY 7TH

Went to town this morning and got some sulphur to cure the camp itch.

After dinner I went up to General Vaughn's headquarters on business. Had a long talk with the General and Major Stephens, who has just returned from East Tennessee.

This being our night to go to the trenches we went out at dark. I slept in Major Hoyle's room.

The CONFEDERATE RECEIPT BOOK *offered an improved cure for camp itch: "Take iodide of potassium, sixty grains, lard, two ounces, mix well, and after washing the body well with warm soap suds rub the ointment over the person three times a week. In seven or eight days the acarus or itch insect will be destroyed. In this recipe the horrible effects of the old sulphur ointment are obviated."*[9] *The most important ingredient of either cure was undoubtedly the admonition to wash regularly.*

FRIDAY, MAY 8TH

Had nothing of particular interest today. I confidently expected a letter but none came.

SATURDAY, MAY 9TH

Got up this morning just in time for breakfast. The weather has turned quite warm again.

Captain and I went up to see Miss Emma this morning but found she was staying in town.

This afternoon I walked over to the brigade Commissary to get some sugar but did not succeed. No mail for me today.

Sunday, May 10th.

Was a bright warm day. The first half of my day was spent in reading my Bible, and after becoming quite weary—and awfully afflicted with the blues—I started a letter to Cousin Maggie. The blues got the upper hand of me so that I had to quit.

In the afternoon I attended preaching in the regiment. Rev. James H. Alexander—a young Presbyterian minister—officiated and gave us an interesting sermon.

Monday, May 11th

As soon as breakfast was over, Captain Wash and I went over to the brigade commissary to get something to eat, but as the sugar had not arrived, we determined to wait. Rowed around in a boat for a while, but found it rather warm work.

Succeeded in getting 100 pounds of sugar for our mess, the greater portion of which I thought to send home if we could get some more anyway soon.

Was somewhat disappointed in not finding a letter for me on my return.

Tuesday, May 12th

Spent the early portion of the day in reading and looking around and reading a little.

About one o'clock we were ordered to cook rations in a hurry and at four A.M. were ordered to march in the direction of Jackson; where we were to stop, no one knew. About ten o'clock we turned in for the night about six miles from camp, having been delayed in starting and marched slowly. Slept in the open air very soundly.

Vaughn's brigade had been ordered to Mount Alban, to reinforce General Bowen at Bovina, if needed.[10]

WEDNESDAY, MAY 13TH

Started on our way this morning about three o'clock. After a weary march we were halted at Big Black Bridge and ordered to await further orders at that place. Were assigned a position in the trenches at that place.

After the war, Col. James G. Rose, who commanded the Sixty-first Regiment at Big Black, wrote a history of his regiment for inclusion in THE MILITARY ANNALS OF TENNESSEE. *In it he claims that the brigade was not positioned at the river until three days later, "in the evening of May 16 ... occupying a line of unfinished earth-works." The defensive line was undoubtedly better prepared than this description implies, and in any case Rose does not mention the three days that his troops had to improve upon it.*[11]

THURSDAY, MAY 14TH

Remained in the trenches all day without the slightest shelter from rain or sun. The morning was oppressively warm. In the evening a very heavy rain fell which gave us all a good drenching. After it was over I got to a house where I was partially dried before night.

FRIDAY, MAY 15TH

We were ordered to move forward five miles this evening with our regiment leaving the rest of the brigade behind. We reached our destination (Edwards Depot) about sundown, and bivouacked in open field.

On this day, General Pemberton ordered General Vaughn to send up one regiment to act as an advance guard at Edwards Depot.[12]

SATURDAY, MAY 16TH (NEAR BAKERS CREEK)

This is my twenty first birthday and was ushered in with the roar of artillery.

About ten o'clock A.M. the firing was terrific on our left and continued until about three in the evening, prisoners coming in all the time. At this time the stragglers commenced arriving and then came the wagon train in a perfect rush. I knew what was up. We were falling back—but in pretty good order.

Our company was posted on the rail road to stop stragglers but they came so fast we had quite a time of it. At length the enemy came right up in sight when one of General Pemberton's staff ordered us to Big Black Bridge—here we were posted for the same purpose as the evening before. Remained on duty all night.

The firing John Earnest heard was the battle at Champion Hill.

SUNDAY, MAY 17TH

We made a stand at the Big Black—the enemy moved forward and opened on us at sunrise. The fight was heavy until about ten o'clock, when the enemy turned our left flank and forced us to retire. Then commenced a pel mel retreat.

We had a foot race to Vicksburg. I at length arrived at our old camp—completely broken down and nearly strangling for water.

In the fight on the other side of the river when we fell back our regiment was so far in advance on the right that they found it impossible to reach the bridge. Only two companies (ours, K, and Captain Bachman's, G) escaped, together with a few stragglers. The rest were all killed or captured.[13]

After resting for near three hours we were ordered below town and marched nearly all night before we could find out where the brigade was.

MONDAY, MAY 18TH

From Monday May 18th to Saturday July 4th we were besieged in Vicksburg. During this time we endured as much as mortals ever endured in an army—every day from daylight until late in the night—sometimes all night, we were in the midst of hissing shells and balls of every character that were ever manufactured. Beside this, we lived on less than quarter rations—ate pea bread, mule meat, and rats.

Finally on the 4th of July we were forced to surrender for the want of something to eat, our rations having given out and we being surrounded by an enemy five times our number—precluding all hope of cutting out.

John Earnest had carefully entered the date for his next entry, on May 18, but was clearly disheartened by the march of events and did not record details of the siege. His final entry, above, is a bleak summary of the fall of Vicksburg.

Notes

Preface

1. Edwin C. Bearss writes, "In my eleven years at Vickburg it was impossible to find a single primary document telling of eating rats, although statements to that effect appear in some histories. The origin of the rat story is with men of several Louisiana regiments who ate muskrats. Indeed, these men were eating muskrats before the investment." Nye, *Struggle for Vicksburg,* 55 n.

Part I. Biographies

JOHN GUILFORD EARNEST

1. Stevenson, *Increase in Excellence,* 90–91.
2. McKenzie, "Civil War and Socioeconomic Change," 172.
3. Bryan, *East Tennessee,* 19.
4. Ibid., 23.
5. Ibid., 53.
6. Groce, *Mountain Rebels,* 6, 40.
7. Bryan, *East Tennessee,* 16 n. 10.
8. *Official Records,* ser. 1, 4:511. (hereafter cited as *O.R.*)

9. Bryan, *East Tennessee,* 23.

10. Groce, *Mountain Rebels,* 91.

11. A. F. Naff to John H. Crawford, September 9, 1862, Paul M. Fink Collection.

12. C. A. Evans, *Confederate Military History,* 10:681.

13. Harvey L. Chase, answer to Question 41. *Tennessee Civil War Questionnaires,* Roll 2.

14. Lindsley, *Military Annals of Tennessee,* 2:576.

15. Letter from Antique American Firearms, referring to National Archives Record Group 94.

16. *O.R.,* ser. 1, 38, pt. 1:850.

17. The last mention of Earnest in the *Compiled Service Records,* Record Group 109, Roll 338, is a regimental return for October 1864 recording him as present. The records of the Confederate Records and Pension Office in Atlanta, Georgia, list Earnest as "Surrendered, Christiansburg, Virginia, April 1865."

18. Robertson, *Soldiers Blue and Gray,* 156.

19. Garrett, *Atlanta and Its Environs,* 2:829.

20. Clark, *Valleys of the Shadow,* 60.

21. "The forced exile of Confederates was relatively short in duration." McKenzie, *One South or Many?* 107. Nevertheless, the absence of active persecution may not have translated to the acceptance necessary to permit the building of a profitable medical practice.

22. Copy of directory in possession of the editor. The first telephone exchange in Atlanta began operation in 1879 with fifty-five subscribers. Garrett, *Yesterday's Atlanta,* 41.

23. Garrison, "Dixie Memories."

John C. Vaughn and His Brigade

1. *O.R.,* ser. 1, 2:945.
2. Ibid.
3. Groce, *Mountain Rebels,* 80.
4. Ibid., 94.
5. Ibid., 93.
6. Bryan, *East Tennessee,* 100. *O.R.,* ser. 1, 10, pt. 1:20–21.

7. *O.R.*, ser. 1, 20, pt. 2:462.

8. *O.R.*, ser. 1, 17, pt. 1: 671, 673–74.

9. *O.R.*, ser. 1, 17, pt. 1:665–69.

10. Any failure of Johnston and Davis to agree on strategy here was undoubtedly aggravated by an ongoing feud between the two men. Biographers of each tend to place the blame on the other (see for example, Eaton, *Jefferson Davis,* and Symonds, *Joseph E. Johnston*), but there can be no doubt that at the least the two had some difficulty in communicating effectively with one another.

11. *O.R.,* ser. 1, 24, pt. 1:325, 327.

12. Sources differ as to the number of troops available to Pemberton. This account relies on the estimate of Bearss, *Campaign for Vicksburg,* 2:563–64.

13. Bearss, *Campaign for Vicksburg,* 2:637.

14. Foote, *Civil War,* 2:377.

15. Bearss, *Campaign for Vicksburg,* 2:678.

16. *O.R.,* ser. 1, 24:267.

17. Lindsley, *Military Annals of Tennessee,* 2:575.

18. Ibid.

19. Foote, *Civil War,* 2:408.

20. Bearss, *Campaign for Vicksburg,* 3:1283.

21. Groce, *Mountain Rebels,* 103.

22. *O.R.,* ser. 2, 6:113.

23. *O.R.,* ser. 1, 31, pt. 3:581–82.

24. *O.R.,* ser. 1, 31, pt. 3:871–72.

25. *O.R.,* ser. 1, 31, pt. 1:12.

26. *O.R.,* ser. 1, 31, pt. 3:889, 891.

27. *O.R.,* ser. 1, 32, pt. 3:845–46; ser. 1, 17, pt. 2:814.

28. *O.R.,* ser. 1, 32, pt. 3:845.

29. Johnston, "Sketches of Operations," 319.

30. Brice, *Conquest of a Valley,* 80.

31. *O.R.,* ser. 1, 37, pt. 1: 764–65.

32. Brice, *Campaign for Vicksburg,* 131.

33. *O.R.,* ser. 1, 49, pt. 1:866.

34. *O.R.,* ser. 1, 49, pt. 1:974.

35. *O.R.,* ser. 1, 49, pt. 1:990–91.

36. *O.R.,* ser. 1, 49, pt. 2:413–14.

37. C. A. Evans, *Confederate Military History,* 10:341; Johnson and Buel, *Battles and Leaders,* 4:764.

38. *O.R.,* ser. 1, 49, pt. 2:687.

39. T. Evans, *Thomas County,* 1:373.

Part II. The Diary of John Guilford Earnest

CHAPTER 1. FROM EAST TENNESSEE TO VICKSBURG

1. Samuel Rhea Gammon was captain of Company B, Sixtieth Tennessee. It has not been possible to identify all persons mentioned by Earnest in his diary. For men serving in Vaughn's brigade, including Captain Gammon, the primary reference is National Record Group 109, *Compiled Service Records of Confederate Units.* That record covers the period September 1862–October 1864. Ranks given in these notes are the highest attained during that period. Other compilations that have been useful are included in the bibliography.

2. *Compiled Service Records,* M861, Roll 55.

3. "Whistled off the rubbers," meaning "to take off the brakes of a railway engine," is a term that was obsolete by the end of the nineteenth century.

4. This entry is incorrectly dated; Friday was in fact November 21. Earnest continues the error until December 1. The dates in this edition have been corrected.

5. Captain H. B. Latrobe commanded the Third Maryland Battery. *O.R.,* ser. 1, 2, pt. 2:414.

6. John Earnest's twenty-five-year-old cousin, J. Tate Earnest, was a private in Company I of the Sixtieth and an assistant surgeon of the Sixtieth Tennessee. William D. Rankin was assistant commissary, subsistence. *Compiled Service Records*, Record Group 109, Roll 338. The 1860 Census for Whitfield County, Georgia, Dalton District, records L. W. Earnest, merchant and farmer, as reporting Inez E. and Martha E. Waugh, aged fourteen and twelve, as members of his household, as well as his wife and five children, the oldest of whom was eleven.

7. Black, *Railroads of the Confederacy,* 17.

8. James Alexander Rhea, later lieutenant colonel of the Sixtieth Tennessee.

9. Davis, *Diary of a Confederate Soldier,* 76.

10. Wiley, *Life of Johnny Reb,* 40.

11. *O.R.,* ser. 1, 17, pt. 2:773.

12. Black, *Railroads of the Confederacy,* 6, 74, 169.

13. Rogers, *Confederate Home Front,* 52.

14. Jones, "A Georgia Confederate Soldier," 106.

15. Probably A. N. Harris, surgeon of the Sixtieth Tennessee.

16. John M. Morrow, captain, Company K, Sixtieth Tennessee.

17. In his response to the 1860 Census, A. F. Posey, age thirty-nine, described himself as a land agent. The Merrell family has not been identified.

18. At this time there was no bridge across Mobile Bay nor a decent road through the swampy land surrounding its upper reaches. Shortly after the fall of Vicksburg, ferry steamers were modified to accommodate rail cars, and equipment that could no longer be used in Mississippi was moved east. Black, *Railroads of the Confederacy,* 170.

19. The 1860 Census gives Jackson's population as 3,191; according to one history of the city, the population of Knoxville was 5,300. Deadrick, *Heart of the Valley,* 74.

20. In 1858, the New Orleans, Jackson & Great Northern Rairoad began running the 206 miles from New Orleans to Canton, where it connected with the Mississippi Central. Black, *Railroads of the Confederacy,* 8.

21. An order from General Pemberton in Granada, dated December 17, 1862, directed that Vaughn's brigade, "just arrived at this point, will report to the command of Major General Maury," *O.R.,* ser. 1, 17, pt. 2:799.

22. On December 23, 1862, General Pemberton ordered: "Brigadier-General Vaughn's brigade is relieved from duty with General Maury's division, and will proceed with all dispatch to Vicksburg, Miss., and report to Major-General Smith." *O.R.,* ser. 1, 17, pt. 2:803.

23. *O.R.,* ser. 1, 17, pt. 1:666, 678.

24. Walker, *Vicksburg: A People at War,* 3–12, describes Vicksburg on the eve of battle.

25. William Allen Wash, captain, Company I, Sixtieth Tennessee.

26. Probably Thomas T. Bouldin, first lieutenant, Company I, Sixtieth Tennessee.

27. The artillery company commanded by Capt. John Peyton Lynch was organized in East Tennessee on December 21, 1861. After the fall of Vicksburg it served with Vaughn in East Tennessee and southwestern Virginia for the rest of the war. Civil War Centennial Commission, *Tennesseans in the Civil War,* 1:134–35.

CHAPTER 2. WAITING IN THE TRENCHES

1. This was probably James B. Pitts, surgeon of the Sixty-first Regiment. As noted in the next entry, the regiment's colonel also preached.

2. Col. Fountain E. Pitts was commander of the Sixty-first Tennessee; an elderly minister, he resigned on May 1, 1863. Lindsley, *Military Annals of Tennessee,* 2:574.

3. Grant, "Fred Grant as a Boy with the Army," 12.

4. At the time of the 1860 Census, E. W. Cade was fifty-five years old, with six children. By 1863, the oldest son, not mentioned by Earnest, was about twenty-five and presumably in the service. Will would have been about twenty-two in 1863 and the Misses Cynthia and Ann sixteen and fourteen.

5. Emily Leavell acknowledged her age as forty-five in 1860. By 1863, her daughter Matilda would have been about twenty-seven, and George around twenty-one.

6. John H. Crouch, captain, Company C, Sixtieth Tennessee.

7. "Janes" is a variant spelling of jeans. The name of the fabric is supposed to derive from a cloth first woven in Genoa, Italy, with "Genoese" over centuries being transformed to jeans. Levi Strauss had peddled these inexpensive pants in Kentucky before the war and before he made his way to San Francisco and became famous for his denim Levi's. Cray, *Levi's,* 22–23.

8. Richard Bowman to Joseph Bowman, March 18, 1863, Bowman Family Collection.

9. The spire of St. Paul's Church and the cupola of the courthouse were the dominant features of Vicksburg's skyline. St. Paul's was destroyed

by a tornado in 1953. However, it and its surviving sister church in Natchez, St. Mary's, built around the same time, are said to have been designed to be very much alike in appearance. Columbiads were one of several types of cannon in use at Vicksburg.

10. W. E. Hunt, first lieutenant, Company K, Sixtieth Tennessee.

11. First published in 1859. Mayne Reid (1818–83) was a popular British writer of boy's adventure stories.

12. Nicholas Fain, second lieutenant, Company B, Sixtieth Tennessee. Jake Miller has not been identified.

13. Azel Stevens Roe (1798–1886). First published in 1855.

14. The deceased was S. F. Ray, second lieutenant, Company K, Sixtieth Tennessee. William Ray, also second lieutenant, in the same company, returned after his melancholy trip and died at Vicksburg on June 18, 1863.

15. Following this entry there are three and one-half pages headed "Miscellaneous Notes on Latin." The opening sentence will be sufficient to illustrate the whole: "*Ratio* = ones own choice, or the well digested reflection of the understanding: it is opposed to *fors* = the mere chance or accident." In addition to the Latin notes, there are more than two pages of "Notes on Greek given to the class . . ." following the entry for April 28.

16. Booth, *Records of Louisiana Confederate Soldiers,* 2:76.

17. Captain Neale has not been identified. The other roommate may have been Oliver P. Martin, first lieutenant, Company D, Sixtieth Tennessee.

18. In the 1860 Census, S. B. Wall identified himself as a farmer, originally from Virginia. His daughter Martha was twenty-three at that time.

19. Steiner, *Disease in the Civil War,* 16, 222–23.

20. C. S. Newman, adjutant, Sixtieth Regiment.

21. Frank S. Blair, captain, Company A, Sixtieth Tennessee.

22. Robertson, *Soldiers Blue and Gray,* 157.

23. In the 1860 Slave Census, Samuel Wall reported fifteen adult slaves, including two males age seventy-three. One of these may have been the wily Uncle Wesley.

24. Nathan Gregg, later colonel, Sixtieth Regiment.

25. John A. Conley, second lieutenant, Company K, Sixtieth Tennessee. He is noted in *Compiled Service Records* as retired, February 23, 1863.

26. John A. Rowan was colonel, Sixty–second Tennessee.

27. The *Hartford* was the flagship of Adm. David G. Farragut, operating on the Mississippi below Vicksburg.

28. Admiral Porter, commanding the Union fleet above Vicksburg, attempted to reinforce Admiral Farragut's fleet below the city by sending two boats, *Switzerland* and *Lancaster,* down past the batteries. The *Lancaster* sank, but the heavily damaged *Switzerland* made the passage and was patched up and returned to service. Bearss, *Campaign for Vicksburg,* 1:696–98.

29. William H. Crawford, chaplain, Sixty–first Tennessee; George W. Renfroe, chaplain, Sixty–second Tennessee.

30. Perhaps Samuel Spars, first lieutenant, Company B, Sixtieth Tennessee.

31. William E. Allen and W. C. Lotspeich were second lieutenants, Company I, Sixtieth Tennessee.

32. Sergeant Bowman is undoubtedly Alfred Bowman, who had been reported by his brother Richard as "down with the fever" in a March 18 letter to his father. Richard Bowman to Joseph Bowman, March 18, 1863, Bowman Family Collection.

33. Mark Bacon, captain, Company F, and James C. Hodges, captain, Company H, Sixtieth Tennessee.

34. George W. Britt and John A. McBride were second lieutenants in Company H, Sixtieth Tennessee.

35. Thomas A. Stonecipher, second lieutenant, Company C, Sixtieth Tennessee. *White swelling* is an archaic term for tuberculosis of the bone or joints.

36. On April 15, General Pemberton directed, "Prepare Vaughn's brigade to move to Tullahoma" to reinforce General Johnston. The next day, he changed his mind: "Defer the movement of Vaughn's brigade until further orders." *O.R.,* ser. 1, 24, pt. 3:744, 747.

CHAPTER 3. CAMPAIGN AND SIEGE

1. Carter, *The Final Fortress,* 157.

2. "Col. C," John H. Crawford, was succeeded as commander of the Sixtieth Tennessee in 1864 by Nathan Gregg.

3. Mary Jane Holmes (1825–1907). First published in 1856.

4. Carter, *The Final Fortress,* 181–82.

5. Ibid., 182–83.

6. *O.R.,* ser. 1, 17, pt. 1:328.

7. David Nelson, *The Cause and Cure of Infidelity: Including a Notice of the Author's Unbelief and the Means of His Rescue.* First published by the American Tract Society in 1836. In an edition published in the 1890s, the society provided a summary description: "On the cause & cure of atheism, with many references to Scripture passages including those of an eschatological nature, by a physician-surgeon who converted to the Christian faith in mid-life & became a Presbyterian minister."

8. Carnes, "We Can Hold Our Ground," 26.

9. *Confederate Receipt Book,* 22.

10. *O.R.,* ser. 1, 24, pt. 3:862.

11. Lindsley, *Military Annals of Tennessee,* 2:575.

12. *O.R.,* ser. 1, 24, pt. 3:883.

13. J. W. Bachman, captain, Company G, Sixtieth Tennessee; later brigade chaplain.

Bibliography

Bearss, Edwin Cole. *The Campaign for Vicksburg*. 3 vols. Dayton, Ohio: Morningside House, 1985.

Black, Robert C., III. *The Railroads of the Confederacy*. Chapel Hill: Univ. of North Carolina Press, 1952.

Boatner, Mark Mayo, III. *The Civil War Dictionary*. New York: David McKay Co., 1959.

Booth, Andrew B., comp. *Records of Louisiana Confederate Soldiers and Louisiana Confederate Commands*. 3 vols. Spartanburg, S.C.: Reprint Co., 1984.

Bowman Family Collection, Archives of Appalachia, East Tennessee State Univ.

Brice, Marshall M. *Conquest of a Valley*. Charlottesville: Univ. Press of Virginia, 1965.

Brooks, Stewart M. *Civil War Medicine*. Springfield, Ill.: Charles C. Thomas, 1966.

Bryan, Charles F. "East Tennessee in the Civil War." Ph.D. diss., Univ. of Tennessee, 1978.

———. "'Tories' Amidst Rebels: Confederate Occupation of East Tennessee, 1861–1863." *East Tennessee Historical Society Publications* 60 (1988): 3–22.

Carnes, F. G. "We Can Hold Our Ground: The Diary of Calvin M. Smith, Lieut., 31st Tenn." *Civil War Times Illustrated* 24, no. 2 (Apr. 1985): 24–66.

Carter, Samuel, III. *The Final Fortress: The Campaign for Vicksburg, 1862–1863.* New York: St. Martin's Press, 1980.

Civil War Centennial Commission. *Tennesseans in the Civil War.* 2 vols. Nashville: Civil War Centennial Commission, 1964.

Clark, Willene B. *Valleys of the Shadow: The Memoir of Confederate Captain Reuben G. Clark.* Knoxville: Univ. of Tennessee Press, 1994.

Cole, Garold L., ed. *Civil War Eyewitnesses: An Annotated Bibliography of Books and Articles, 1955–1986.* Columbia: Univ. of South Carolina Press, 1988.

Confederate Receipt Book: A Compilation of Over One Hundred Receipts, Adapted to the Times. Richmond: West and Johnston, 1863. Republished with introduction by E. Merton Coulter. Athens: Univ. of Georgia Press, 1960.

Cray, Ed. *Levi's.* Boston: Houghton Mifflin Co., 1978.

Cunningham, Horace H. *Doctors in Grey: The Confederate Medical Service.* Baton Rouge: Louisiana State Univ. Press, 1958.

Currie, James T. *Enclave: Vicksburg and Her Plantations, 1863–1870.* Jackson: Univ. Press of Mississippi, 1980.

Davis, William C. *Breckinridge: Statesman, Soldier, Symbol.* Baton Rouge: Louisiana State Univ. Press, 1974.

———. *Diary of a Confederate Soldier: John S. Jackman of the Orphan Brigade.* Columbia: Univ. of South Carolina Press, 1990.

———, ed. *The Confederate Generals.* 6 vols. N.p.: National Historical Society, 1991.

Deadrick, Lucile, ed. *Heart of the Valley, A History of Knoxville Tennessee*. Knoxville: East Tennessee Historical Society, 1976.

Derks, Scott, ed. *The Value of a Dollar: Prices and Income in the United States*. Detroit: Gold Research, 1994.

Eaton, Clement. *Jefferson Davis*. New York: Free Press, 1977.

Evans, Clement A., ed. *Confederate Military History Extended Edition*. 17 vols. Wilmington, N.C.: Broadfoot Publishing Co., 1987.

Evans, Tad. *Thomas County, Georgia, Newspaper Clippings*. 3 vols. Savannah, Ga.: Tad Evans, 1995.

Fisher, Noel C. *War at Every Door: Partisan Politics and Guerrilla Violence in East Tennessee, 1860–1869*. Chapel Hill: Univ. of North Carolina Press, 1997.

Foote, Shelby. *The Civil War: A Narrative*. 3 vols. New York: Random House, 1963.

Freeman, Frank R. *Microbes and Minié Balls: An Annotated Bibliography of Civil War Medicine*. Rutherford, N.J.: Farleigh Dickenson Univ. Press, 1993.

Gallagher, Gary W., ed. *Struggle for the Shenandoah*. Kent, Ohio: Kent State Univ. Press, 1991.

Garrett, Franklin M. *Atlanta and Its Environs*. New York: Lewis Historical Publishing Co., 1954.

———. *Yesterday's Atlanta*. Miami: E. A. Seeman Publishing Co., 1974.

Garrison, Webb. "Dixie Memories." *Atlanta Journal and Constitution*, Sunday, Nov. 2, 1986.

Grabau, Warren E. *Ninety-eight Days: A Geographer's View of the Vicksburg Campaign*. Knoxville: Univ. of Tennessee Press, 2000.

Grant, Frederick D., "Fred Grant as a Boy with the Army." *Confederate Veteran* 16, no. 1 (1908): 10–14.

Groce, W. Todd. "Confederate Faces in East Tennessee." *Journal of East Tennessee History* 65 (1993): 3–33.

————. *Mountain Rebels: East Tennessee Confederates and the Civil War, 1860–1870*. Knoxville: Univ. of Tennessee Press, 1999.

Hewett, Janet B., ed. *The Roster of Confederate Soldiers*. 16 vols. Wilmington, N.C.: Broadfoot Publishing Co., 1996.

Johnson, Robert U., and Clarence C. Buel, eds. *Battles and Leaders of the Civil War*. 4 vols. New York: Century Co., 1884.

Johnston, J. Stoddard. "Sketches of Operations of General John C. Breckinridge," parts 1–3, *Southern Historical Society Papers* 7, no. 6 (1879): 257–62; no. 7 (1879): 317–23; no. 8 (1879): 385–92.

Jones, Allen W., ed. "A Georgia Confederate Soldier Visits Montgomery, Alabama, 1862–1863." *Alabama Historical Quarterly* 25 (1963): 99–113.

Korn, Jerry. *War on the Mississippi: Grant's Vicksburg Campaign*. Alexandria, Va.: Time-Life Books, 1985.

Lenoir, William B. *History of Sweetwater Valley*. Richmond: Presbyterian Committee of Publication, 1916.

Lindsley, John B., ed. *The Military Annals of Tennessee*. 2 vols. Wilmington, N.C.: Broadfoot Publishing Co., 1995.

McBride, Robert M., et al., comps. *Biographical Dictionary of the Tennessee General Assembly*. 4 vols. Nashville: Tennessee Historical Commission, 1979.

McKenzie, Robert Tracy. "Civil War and Socioeconomic Change in the Upper South: The Survival of Local Agricultural Elites in Tennessee, 1850–1870." *Tennessee Historical Quarterly* 52 (1993): 170–84.

————. *One South or Many? Plantation Belt and Upcountry in Civil War–Era Tennessee*. New York: Cambridge Univ. Press, 1994.

Michie, Peter S. *The Life and Letters of Emory Upton*. New York: D. Appleton, 1885.

Napier, John H., III. "Montgomery during the Civil War." *Alabama Review* 46 (Apr. 1988): 103–31.

National Archives, Washington, D.C. Record Group 109. Compiled Service Records of Confederate Units, 1861–1865.

Noe, Kenneth W., and Shannon H. Wilson, eds. *The Civil War in Appalachia: Collected Essays*. Knoxville: Univ. of Tennessee Press, 1997.

Nye, Wilbur S., ed. *Struggle for Vicksburg: The Battles and Siege That Decided the Civil War*. Harrisburg, Pa.: Historical Times, 1967. Reissued by Eastern Acorn Press, 1982.

Paul M. Fink Collection, Tennessee State Library and Archives.

Pemberton, John C. *Pemberton: Defender of Vicksburg*. Chapel Hill: Univ. of North Carolina Press, 1942.

Pomerantz, Gary M. *Where Peachtree Meets Sweet Auburn: The Saga of Two Families and the Making of Atlanta*. New York: Simon & Schuster, 1996.

Robertson, James I., Jr. *Soldiers Blue and Gray*. Columbia: Univ. of South Carolina Press, 1988.

Rogers, William Warren, Jr. *Confederate Home Front: Montgomery during the Civil War*. Tuscaloosa: Univ. of Alabama Press, 1999.

Russell, James M., *Atlanta, 1847–1900: City Building in the Old South and New*. Baton Rouge: Louisiana State Univ. Press, 1988.

Sands, Sarah G. Cox. *History of Monroe County, Tennessee*. Baltimore: Gateway Press, 1982.

Sifakis, Stewart, ed. *Compendium of the Confederate Armies*. 10 vols. New York: Facts on File, 1992.

Simpson, Brooks D. *Ulysses S. Grant: Triumph over Adversity, 1822–1865*. Boston: Houghton Mifflin, 2000.

Steiner, Paul E. *Disease in the Civil War*. Springfield, Ill.: Charles C. Thomas, 1968.

Stevenson, George J. *Increase in Excellence, A History of Emory and Henry College*. New York: Appleton-Century-Crofts, 1963.

Street, James, Jr. *The Struggle for Tennessee: Tupelo to Stones River*. Alexandria, Va.: Time-Life Books, 1985.

Symonds, Craig L. *Joseph E. Johnston: A Civil War Biography*. New York: W. W. Norton & Co., 1992.

Bibliography

Tennessee Civil War Questionnaires, Tennessee State Library and Archives.

Turner, George E. *Victory Rode the Rails: The Strategic Place of Railroads in the Civil War*. Indianapolis: Bobbs-Merrill, 1953.

U.S. Congress. *A Compilation of the Official Records of the Union and Confederate Navies in the War of the Rebellion*. 31 vols. Washington, D.C., 1894–1927.

U.S. Congress. *War of the Rebellion: A Compilation of the Official Records of the Union and Confederate Armies*. 70 vols. Washington, D.C., 1880–1901.

U.S. Dept. of the Army, Office of the Surgeon General. *Medical and Surgical History of the Civil War*. 15 vols. Wilmington, N.C.: Broadfoot Publishing Co., 1991. Formerly titled *The Medical and Surgical History of the War of the Rebellion (1861–1865)*.

Walker, Peter F. *Vicksburg: A People at War, 1860–1865*. Chapel Hill: Univ. of North Carolina Press, 1960.

Wheeler, Richard. *The Siege of Vicksburg*. New York: Thomas Y. Crowell Co., 1978.

Wiley, Bell Irvin. *The Life of Johnny Reb*. New York: Bobbs-Merrill Co., 1943.

Winschel, Terence J. "The Guns at Champion Hill." *Journal of Confederate History* 6 (1990): 94–105.

Woodworth, Steven E. *Jefferson Davis and His Generals*. Lawrence: Univ. Press of Kansas, 1990.

Index

Index

Index

ALL RIGHT LET THEM COME was designed and typeset on a Macintosh computer system using QuarkXPress software. The body text is set in 11/14 Granjon. This book was designed and typeset by Bill Adams and manufactured by Thomson-Shore, Inc.